Ain't Scared of Your Jail

New Perspectives on the History of the South

UNIVERSITY PRESS OF FLORIDA

Florida A&M University, Tallahassee
Florida Atlantic University, Boca Raton
Florida Gulf Coast University, Ft. Myers
Florida International University, Miami
Florida State University, Tallahassee
New College of Florida, Sarasota
University of Central Florida, Orlando
University of Florida, Gainesville
University of North Florida, Jacksonville
University of South Florida, Tampa
University of West Florida, Pensacola

Ain't Scared of Your Jail

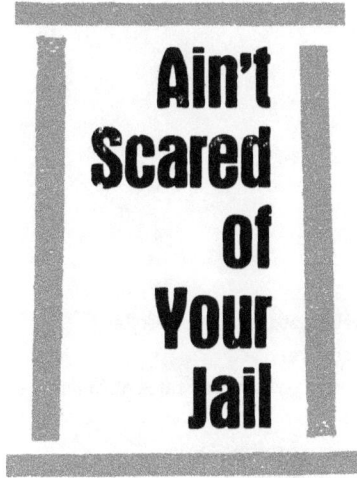

Arrest, Imprisonment, and the Civil Rights Movement

Zoe A. Colley

University Press of Florida
Gainesville · Tallahassee
Tampa · Boca Raton
Pensacola · Orlando · Miami
Jacksonville · Ft. Myers · Sarasota

First cloth printing, 2013
First paperback printing, 2014

Library of Congress Cataloging-in-Publication Data

Colley, Zoe A.
Ain't scared of your jail : arrest, imprisonment, and the civil rights movement / Zoe
A. Colley.
p. cm. -- (New perspectives on the history of the South)
Includes bibliographical references and index.
ISBN 978-0-8130-4241-1 (cloth: alk. paper)
ISBN 978-0-8130-6035-4 (pbk.)
1. Civil rights--United States. 2. African Americans--Civil rights--History--20th
century. 3. Civil rights movements--United States. I. Title. II. Series: New
perspectives on the history of the South.
E185.615.C6434 2013
323.1196'073--dc23
2012031679

University Press of Florida
15 Northwest 15th Street
Gainesville, FL 32611-2079
http://www.upf.com

To Mike

Contents

Acknowledgments

This work grew out of research at the University of Newcastle. I was funded by the Strang Studentship from Newcastle University, as well as a six-month fellowship at the Institute of Historical Research in London. My research in the United States was made possible by grants from the Studentship and Fellowships Committee and the History Department at Newcastle University, the British Association for American Studies, and the Royal Historical Society. More recently, I also received support from the University of St. Andrews, the University of Dundee, the Carnegie Institute for Scottish Universities, and Duke University. My thanks go also to those who agreed to oral history interviews and to the many archivists who assisted me while I was in the United States.

I have been fortunate to work with John Howard. He was, and has continued to be, a great source of support. My thanks to the Department of History at the University of Dundee for its support, in particular Jim Tomlinson and Callum Brown for their comments on drafts of this work.

My deepest gratitude goes to my family and friends for putting up with me and "the book" over the past few years. My husband, Andrew, has helped me in every way possible and in ways I could never repay. My daughters, Alyssa and Lauren, have been an endless source of laughter and cuddles. My Mum and Dad have always supported me in everything I have done, and for this I am forever grateful. My sister, Lynsey, has been a wonderful source of support and friendship over the years. Finally, I never imagined when I started this project that my brother, Michael, would not be here to see it finished. This book is dedicated to him.

Introduction

On the morning of December 11, 1961, civil rights activist Dr. William Anderson sat down with his family to eat breakfast at home in Albany, Georgia. He was president of the newly formed Albany Movement, an organization established to lead the local black community in protest against segregation and discriminatory employment practices. That morning he explained to his family that the movement was about to undertake a series of mass demonstrations, and that he expected to be in jail by the end of the week. In an interview, he later recalled how difficult it had been to break that news to his family. "You'd have to understand that going to jail was probably one of the most feared things in rural Georgia," he recalled. "There were many blacks who were arrested in small towns in Georgia never to be heard from again. We have every reason to believe many of these were lynched. So going to jail was no small thing. It was nothing to be taken lightly by any black."[1] In communities across the South during the 1950s and 1960s, African Americans faced the same difficult decision: to participate in the civil rights movement, they had to accept the likelihood of arrest and imprisonment and, as Anderson understood, that decision was fraught with danger.

Anderson's fear of imprisonment was well-founded. The criminal justice system in the South played a central role in white segregationists' efforts to maintain black social, political, and economic inferiority, and had done so for almost a century. In the midst of the post-emancipation chaos of the late 1860s and 1870s, the criminal justice system—reconstructed by white communities to enable suppression of challenges to the racial status quo—had emerged as a central part of state and local government's campaign to bring the black population back under white control. As Gail Williams O'Brien has demonstrated with great skill, the southern criminal justice system derived its power from the way in which it prioritized the protection of white supremacy over all other issues.[2] From arbitrary police brutality to the complicity of legal officials in acts of lynching, every aspect of this system reminded black communities that they had no claim to legal protection. This was a highly effective and ruthless tool with which white communities controlled black lives; it represented one of the strongest symbols of black powerlessness in the South. Generations of abuse by white legal officials left a deeply ingrained fear of "the law" within the minds of most African Americans.[3]

While some of the worst abuses of the southern criminal justice system were eliminated during the 1940s and 1950s, it remained a staunch guardian of white supremacy. Civil rights activists had long been a target of legal officials, but the increasingly organized and militant style of civil rights protest during those decades made legal repression ever more central to the preservation of white supremacy in the South and, for those who engaged in activism during these years, the criminalization of black protest could be a deeply destructive process. The example of New Iberia, Louisiana, during the latter years of World War II provides evidence of how legal officials often spearheaded campaigns to destroy civil rights activism. A new NAACP (National Association for the Advancement of Colored People) chapter was founded in the town in 1943. Focusing upon voter registration, education provision, and employment rights, the NAACP launched an assault upon the white power structure. In 1944, a black representative of the Fair Employment Practices Committee arrived in town, acting on a complaint about the lack of industrial training for local African Americans. A welding school was subsequently established, much to the chagrin of the local white community, and after a series of confrontations, the NAACP branch president, J. Leo Hardy, was arrested and ordered to leave town by 10 p.m. the next day. When he failed to follow the sheriff's orders, he was bundled into a police car and driven out of town, where he was badly beaten and told to leave New Iberia. This was just the beginning of a series of expulsions of NAACP leaders and black professionals, all overseen by Sheriff Ozenne and his deputies.[4] While a chapter of the NAACP continued to function in New Iberia, it did not return to its previous level of militancy. Adam Fairclough's account of the New Iberia affair makes it clear that the expulsions were controlled by local and state officials, who placed responsibility for executing their plans upon the shoulders of local law enforcement personnel. New Iberia reflects both the importance of the police as guardians of white supremacy and their role as determined adversaries of organized civil rights protest. It was a pattern of police harassment and violence, designed to intimidate and isolate key figures of local protest movements, that was repeated across the South during the 1940s and 1950s.

Although movement contemporaries routinely acknowledged the importance of the jail experience during the 1950s and 1960s, civil rights historians have offered only a cursory review of the developing role of arrest and imprisonment within the movement.[5] Histories often refer to incidences of arrest, trial, and imprisonment, but they tend to reduce civil rights prisoners to mere numbers while also failing to venture past the jailhouse door. Thus, civil rights historians have failed to appreciate how the debate over imprisonment filtered through and shaped the movement's progression. Civil rights protesters did not stop their battle against white supremacy when they went to jail—they took the movement inside the cell and continued the struggle. Despite their isolation, they turned the jail into a physical and symbolic battleground for the movement, and it is only by isolating the question of jail, and by examining this transformation, that one can appreciate its significance. In doing so, this book has two aims. Firstly, it considers the personal experiences of civil rights prisoners. Although the movement made going to jail a collective act, it remained a deeply personal experience. Many things shaped how an individual interpreted their imprisonment: race, gender, age, class, or whether one was from the North or the South. Where some found imprisonment to be an energizing or inspiring experience, others struggled to find a positive value. While emphasizing and exploring these individual experiences, this book also seeks to place them in the context of broader developments within the movement. The question of how to respond to imprisonment was a hotly contested issue, the subject of intense inter- and intraorganizational debate at both the local and national level. Furthermore, reactions to imprisonment were in a constant state of flux, and responded to developments both inside and outside the movement. Therefore, a second point of inquiry is to survey the evolution of attitudes toward arrest and imprisonment within the civil rights movement as a whole.

The following six chapters highlight a number of broad trends within the history of the movement. Perhaps the most important theme to arise from this study is the relationship between mass arrest and the development of the movement's protest tactics. Historians writing since the 1990s have stressed the level of continuity between the pre- and post-1955 periods; however, it is clear from this study that responses to mass arrest brought a sharp break with tradition beginning in the late 1950s. Never before had jails filled to bursting with civil rights activists. Perhaps of even greater importance was the development of an ideology that celebrated jail-going as a liberating and honorable experience. This was a new and radical departure for black protest. Although nonviolent protest in itself was far from new—it had been employed by African Americans on many occasions prior to the 1950s—the element of mass imprisonment, and an ideology that actively promoted incarceration, was absent until the 1950s. One should, however, add a caveat to that argument: although mass imprisonment of African Americans had never been seen before the 1950s, we can nevertheless see ways in which pre-1955 protests influenced this development. Indeed, here is another theme that arises throughout the following chapters. Responses to mass arrest were directly related to African Americans' experience of brutality and injustice at the hands of legal officials. What started as an act of Gandhian resistance was shaped and given meaning by many years of battling against a color-coded criminal justice system.

Historians such as Edward Ayers, Mary-Ellen Curtin, and Gail Williams O'Brien have explored the diverse range of tactics that African Americans used to challenge their treatment by police, courts, and prison authorities.[6] It is clear from such studies that ordinary African Americans, from the streets to the prison, sought to utilize whatever resources they had to improve their treatment. This included groups such as the NAACP working to defend victims of legal injustice, but it also included individual acts of protest. Open resistance was a last resort, and more likely to bring death than any appreciable relief. Alternative strategies included letter-writing, appeals to civil rights organizations for assistance, and use of the courts to challenge unfair treatment. From the Reconstruction era and beyond, the battle against the discriminatory criminal justice system was a central part of the freedom struggle. However, one of the strongest messages from recent research on this subject is that resistance rarely succeeded in bringing about any meaningful systemic change. For the most part, the southern criminal justice system remained as repressive in 1955 as it had been twenty years before. Indeed, as noted earlier, the World War II era marked a severe downturn in police treatment of African Americans which only showed signs of improving toward the end of the decade.

As William Anderson observed, the civil rights movement faced a great challenge in asking African Americans to overcome their fear of imprisonment and risk arrest.[7] However, there were other reasons to avoid jail. The criminalization of African Americans had helped to produce a perception—which was particularly strong among the middle class activists—that going to jail was a deeply shameful experience. Journalist Pat Watters commented upon this form of class division in *Down to Now*: there was a "Negro southern code which distinguished the middle-class not so much in economic terms (for nearly everyone was poor), but by such criteria as whether or not one had been to jail."[8] For many members of the black middle class, the potential loss of status from a criminal record could be a great barrier to involvement in the movement. The role of class in shaping the civil rights jail experience, and responses to mass arrest more generally, arise throughout the course of this book. It is an important factor to consider, not least because the impact of class divisions and identities does not always figure in existing civil rights studies.

The role of gender within the movement has been considered in much greater depth by historians. The contribution of women, their treatment, and, more recently, the construction of masculinity form a strong part of civil rights studies. Just as class helped shape the civil rights jail experience, so too did gender. The proportion of female participants jailed varied, depending on the nature of the individual campaign. As Charles Payne has observed, women often formed the backbone of community-based campaigns. It is clear from looking at some of those campaigns that women also comprised a sizeable proportion of those incarcerated. In other areas, for example the 1964 Freedom Summer, women were exposed to the jail cell less often than men. This was presumably a product of the tendency to consign women to less dangerous tasks such as teaching and administrative work, which were also viewed as most appropriate for women.[9] Nevertheless, as the following chapters demonstrate, women did face violence in the jail cell, and it could be as extreme as that faced by men.

One of the most interesting aspects of the civil rights jail experience is the way in which imprisonment often brought activists into very close contact with the mainstream jail population. Even though civil rights activists were acutely aware of the color-coded nature of the criminal justice system, they often failed to understand just how cruel it was, until it was inflicted upon them. These encounters were instrumental in breaking down the stereotypical views that activists sometimes held of those who were incarcerated. The nature of these encounters and the impact upon both groups are detailed at various points in the following chapters. In doing so, this book highlights the shifting relationship between the movement, the black criminal class, and the southern criminal justice system.

Although civil rights organizations often expressed horror at the conditions in which their members were incarcerated, the movement as a whole tended to avoid focusing upon such matters as a point of protest during the early 1960s. Rather, they generally preferred to focus upon concerns outside the prison and jail system: employment rights, desegregation, and voter registration. As the roots of white supremacy were exposed during the 1960s, and more of their members suffered at the hands of legal authorities, organizations began to incorporate a critique of the legal system into their protest efforts. Consequently, we see an increasing commitment to challenging the conditions in which all prisoners, but especially African Americans, were held. There is evidence that the imprisonment of civil rights activists pushed critiques of the prison system to the fore as early as the 1961 Freedom Rides. By the mid-1960s, many organizations had started to stress the common ground between civil rights and "ordinary" prisoners. In the longer term, the jail experiences of activists helped bring prison reform to the forefront of civil rights activism.

The one organization that had already established itself as a major force in improving the treatment of African American prisoners was the NAACP. This, along with its preference for challenging racism through the courts, set it apart from the other national organizations that were active during the 1960s. Until relatively recently, the NAACP had been either overlooked or portrayed as a backward-looking, conservative force among the more militant organizations of the 1960s. Describing this as a type of "historical amnesia," Adam Fairclough has argued that the NAACP acted as "the backbone of the civil rights struggle."[10] Community and state studies have demonstrated the central role the NAACP played in establishing the grassroots activism upon which the protests of the 1960s were based. This study likewise highlights the contribution of the NAACP, although from a rather different angle. By examining the role of arrest and imprisonment, it underscores how the NAACP was a crucial source of legal advice and bail funds, without which nonviolent organizations like SNCC (Student Nonviolent Coordinating Committee), CORE (Congress of Racial Equality), and SCLC (Southern Christian Leadership Conference) would have struggled greatly to mount many of their campaigns. Yet this certainly was not an easy relationship. Since its inception earlier in the century, the NAACP had made the battle against unequal justice a cornerstone of its program. The protest ideology of jail-no-bail, as advocated by SNCC, CORE, and SCLC during the first half of the 1960s, encouraged activists to refuse bail and embrace imprisonment; in both ideological and practical terms, the NAACP was diametrically opposed to such a policy. Indeed, it was *this* aspect of nonviolent protest that troubled the NAACP's leadership more than any other. The influence of such concerns upon the NAACP at all levels, and upon its relationship with other groups, is a theme that arises throughout this study. Looking at the issue from an even wider perspective, it provides an example of the extent to which the question of how to respond to arrest and imprisonment was intertwined with so many other issues within the movement. It appeared at the local and national level, and was a point of debate both within and between the major civil rights organizations.

Finally, this study is as much about the tactics that the white power structure used to suppress civil rights activity as it is about the movement itself. This book contributes to a growing body of literature on white segregationists by highlighting the ways in which authorities sought to destroy the movement via mass arrest and imprisonment. It was these strategies that turned the jail cell into a battleground between segregationists and the movement.[11]

In the years running up to American involvement in World War II, color-coded justice had a devastating effect upon black communities. Lives were lost and families were torn apart at the hands of legal officials bent on protecting white supremacy at all costs. The mass arrest and imprisonment of civil rights activists in the 1960s was a continuation of this system of racial control. Legal officials had been at the forefront of defending white supremacy for generations; it is no surprise that they were central to the white community's response to mass civil rights protest. For some black southerners, the prospect of directly confronting the police, judges, and jailers within their communities was deeply traumatic. As William Anderson explained, for those who chose to join the movement: "Going to jail was probably one of the most feared things."[12] For such individuals, even those who had never been in trouble with the law, shared memories of police violence, wrongful arrest, or lynching made this long history of legal abuse inescapable. The development of a protest ideology that embraced imprisonment as a mark of honor within the nonviolent movement was most important because it facilitated overcoming those shared memories of almost a century of injustice. In doing so, the movement was able to draw upon a strong tradition of individual and collective resistance to the racism of the criminal justice system. It was against this backdrop of police brutality, arbitrary arrest, and legal injustice that an organized mass civil rights movement emerged in the 1950s and 1960s. As the following chapter demonstrates, the very success of the movement depended upon black communities challenging the same police, judges, and prison guards who had beaten suspects, jailed innocent victims, and even murdered those around them.

1

An American Negro Gandhi?

In 1941, Jay Holmes Smith of the Fellowship of Reconciliation (FOR) announced that the organization was undertaking a search for "an American Negro Gandhi" to lead African Americans in a nonviolent battle against racial discrimination. In doing so, he acknowledged that jail would figure as a locus of black protest.[1] Smith recognized that the southern policeman stood at the front line of a campaign to preserve the racial status quo. Open and direct challenges to southern segregation would inevitably be answered with legal repression. Although Smith's grand search failed to identify such an individual, it foresaw both the opportunities and challenges that the movement would face in the 1950s and 1960s.

Few others, besides Smith and his pacifist colleagues in FOR, would have agreed with his vision for the future of civil rights activism. The one exception was FOR's sister organization, the Congress of Racial Equality, which tested such tactics in its Journey of Reconciliation. In 1947, CORE decided to launch the campaign to test compliance with the recent *Morgan v. Virginia* decision ordering the integration of interstate travel. They planned to use an integrated group of sixteen CORE members to challenge segregated seating on buses along a chosen route through Virginia, North Carolina, Tennessee, and Kentucky. They would stop off in towns on the way to give lectures explaining the campaign and the value of nonviolent protest. By the time the protesters returned to Washington, D.C., two weeks later, they had experienced twelve arrests, one incident of violent white resistance, and a number of confrontations with passengers and bus drivers. The project foretold a number of challenges that CORE and other civil rights organizations would face when conducting nonviolent protest in the coming years. Despite its commitment to Gandhian nonviolence, CORE chose to post bail on each of the occasions when its members were arrested. To have done otherwise would have brought the protest to a grinding halt and placed the lives of those in jail in grave danger. The Congress of Racial Equality learned that when faced with the intransigence of the southern criminal justice system, blindly following Gandhian ideology was not always the best course of action. Even so, CORE still had to face the legal repercussions of these arrests. Fortunately for those involved, all of the charges were eventually dropped, with the exception of four protesters who had been sentenced to thirty days on the chain gang in Chapel Hill, North Carolina. As would often be the case with later arrests, CORE found itself an advocate of Gandhian ideology, but it also felt compelled to challenge the convictions in court. That decision forced them to rely for legal assistance upon the NAACP, whose lawyers acted on behalf of CORE on a number of occasions, including an appeal to the North Carolina Supreme Court against the Chapel Hill convictions. It soon became apparent, however, that the NAACP was deeply reluctant to become embroiled in a legal battle on behalf of CORE. In 1949, three of the four men surrendered themselves to state authorities to serve their sentence on the North Carolina chain gang. This was not the first time that civil rights activists had taken their battle inside the prison walls, but the incorporation of imprisonment as an act of protest *in itself* established an important precedent in the history of nonviolent protest.[2]

Despite CORE's sense of achievement, the Journey of Reconciliation had no impact upon the general mood of civil rights activism in the South. Nonviolent direct action remained a relatively underused tactic, with the NAACP's legalistic approach dominating challenges to the Jim Crow South. The wartime repression of black militancy by legal officials had provided ample evidence, if any more were needed, of the destructive power of the police and courts. Under such conditions, the overwhelming consensus was that open confrontation with white segregationists, particularly the police, would be suicidal. Many civil rights activists in the South were already painfully aware of the destructive potential of a racist criminal justice system. It made much more sense to use the courts to challenge segregation than to engage in protest that increased the risk of legal repression and police brutality. As August Meir and Elliott Rudwick have observed, even where nonviolent protest did occur during this time, it was invariably without an ideological basis. The Congress of Racial Equality's example of Gandhian protest simply did not fit with the prevailing conditions and attitude of activists in the region. The proposition that they should encourage individuals to throw themselves into the jaws of the criminal justice system struck many as counterproductive to their efforts. One final obstacle to the use of nonviolence came with the often conservative attitudes of many black southerners, particularly community leaders. In 1943, W.E.B. Du Bois observed that African Americans were not "ready for systematic lawbreaking." Not only would such action be dangerous, but the economic consequences of being arrested, in particular losing one's job, could be disastrous. Furthermore, the argument that one should willingly accept arrest and imprisonment was unlikely to find support among the black middle classes, who traditionally dominated civil rights organizing. They had fought against the stereotypical image of African Americans as lazy, illiterate, and prone to criminal behavior for years, and as such were unlikely to become "jailbirds" themselves.[3]

The story of Rosa Parks's protest against bus segregation in Montgomery, Alabama, and the mass protest that followed is no doubt familiar to many. The remainder of this chapter mines that familiar history for evidence of the way in which city authorities sought to criminalize the boycott, and reflects upon the fact that the criminal justice system was the primary weapon available to them in their efforts to crush the protest. More importantly, perhaps, it also demonstrates how the black community responded to such repression, and how those responses changed and became more defiant as the protest progressed. In particular, it illustrates the way in which gender and class identities shaped those responses.

According to Meier and Rudwick, there was a dramatic shift in the focus of nonviolent protest from the North to the South during the latter half of the 1950s. Their explanation for this lies in the success of the NAACP's legal challenges to segregation, most especially the *Brown v. Board of Education* decision that overturned the legal basis of segregated education in the South, and an increase in black voter registration. These developments heightened black expectations and caused communities to adopt more militant strategies in their challenges of Jim Crow. More recently, historians such as Lance Hill and Timothy Tyson have painted a complex picture of the South in the late 1950s. Their work has highlighted the extent to which nonviolent protest was far from an automatic response for black communities. These years appear as a battleground between advocates of nonviolence and activists who stressed the need for political and economic empowerment alongside self-defense.[4] In this context, the Montgomery Bus Boycott is important for the way in which it reflects the changing circumstances of civil rights activism in the South, but it should not be perceived as a radical turning point in the history of the movement. Nevertheless, it is clear that some important changes in civil rights protest took place during the mid-1950s, and that these were evident in Montgomery.

Arrest was certainly not an unusual experience for those who chose to challenge the color line in the postwar South. As Robin Kelley has shown, individual acts of resistance to southern segregation were a familiar part of southern urban life; while southern African Americans were not yet prepared for *systematic* lawbreaking, challenges to segregation laws nevertheless took place with relative regularity.[5] Those who chose to directly challenge the color line did so with a keen awareness that they were, indirectly, courting arrest. Thus, when Rosa Parks refused to surrender her seat on a Montgomery bus to a white man on December 1, 1955, she engaged in an act of resistance that had been played out numerous times in the South. "As I sat there, I tried not to think about what might happen. I knew that anything was possible. I could be manhandled or beaten." Parks was escorted from the bus by two policemen and placed in a patrol car.[6] At City Hall she was fingerprinted, mug shots were taken, and for the first time she walked into a jail cell. One of the enduring themes in the civil rights jail experience is the way in which imprisonment brought activists into direct contact with "ordinary" black criminals, and this was certainly the case for Rosa Parks. One of her cellmates refused to speak. The other told her she had been in jail for more than six weeks. "She'd been keeping company with another man," Parks recalled, "and he'd got angry with her and struck her. She took a hatchet and went after him, and he had her arrested." The woman was now stuck in jail, unable to raise bail herself and prevented from contacting her brothers to request their help. Her boyfriend wanted to bail her out, but she was unwilling to submit to further domestic violence. Such stories were commonplace inside southern jails. Black, working-class women dominated the female inmate population, and their gender rarely helped them overcome the vehement racism of the criminal justice system.[7]

Parks's first introduction to jail life did not last long. With the help of white lawyer Clifford Durr, her husband secured bail. Members of the Women's Political Council (WPC), an organization of black female Montgomery residents, seized upon Parks's arrest as an opportunity to generate widespread support for a bus boycott.[8] They spent the night mimeographing leaflets which called for a bus boycott the following Monday.[9] To their delight, the protest was a resounding success. Montgomery's buses were virtually empty. The same day, Parks was convicted of violating the city's segregation ordinance and ordered to pay a ten-dollar fine plus court costs.

The arrest and conviction of Rosa Parks—the event that precipitated the boycott—is the most obvious example of the interaction between civil rights activism and the legal system; however, issues relating to arrest and imprisonment circulated throughout the history of the bus boycott and were a central factor in shaping its development. Long before Parks was arrested, Mary Fair Burks, founder of the WPC, had already been politicized by an experience of wrongful arrest and imprisonment. She recalled how she was driving her car "when the traffic light turned green. As I started to accelerate, I saw a white woman attempting to get to the curb. The short of it was that after the woman stopped cursing me, I was arrested." The arresting officer used his billy club to silence Burks's protestations that she had not committed any crime. Although the intervention of a local white lawyer ensured that the charges against Burks were quickly dropped, the experience left her embittered *and* politicized. "It was after this truly traumatic experience that I resolved to do something more about segregation besides waging my own personal war. My arrest convinced me that my defiance alone would do little or nothing to remedy such situations." A few weeks later, having recounted her experience to a group of forty women, the Women's Political Council was founded.[10]

Parks's conviction of violating a municipal ordinance requiring bus segregation opened up the possibility of a direct legal challenge to bus segregation; however, it also had a politicizing impact upon Montgomery's black community.[11] In an interview, Nixon explained how the black community reacted to her trial and conviction:

Mrs. Parks was tried that morning and she was found guilty. . . . I'd been in court off and on for twenty years . . . and very seldom, if ever, there was another black man unless he was being tried. . . . When we got outside, police were standing with sawed-off shotguns, and the people all up and down the streets was [sic] from sidewalk to sidewalk out there. I looked around there, and I bet you there was over a thousand black people—black men—on the streets out there.[12]

In the Jim Crow South, the courthouse symbolized white ownership of the legal system. It was the place where laws were filtered through a racial lens, and sentences imposed according to the color of one's skin. Nixon's observation that Parks's trial drew members of the black community to this site of injustice and repression was not only an act of support for Parks, but also an expression of resistance against the white authorities. Crucially, Nixon picked out the fact that black *men* formed a sizeable proportion of the crowd. Working-class African American men had suffered the burden of police brutality, arrest, and imprisonment for generations. The impact of that history upon black men's behavior in Montgomery was noted by Jo Ann Robinson, a leading member of the WPC: "For, at the first hint of conflict [on the buses], the men left at the nearest exit. . . . The men feared arrest and did not expect to get justice in the courts."[13] Accounts of the arrests of both Parks and Claudette Colvin, who was arrested for refusing to observe segregation on the buses prior to Parks, describe the way in which the black men who were on the bus disembarked one by one as the confrontation grew. Referring to Colvin's refusal to relinquish her seat to a white passenger, Robinson described how "Negro men sensed trouble. With their heavy responsibilities at home, they could ill afford arrest . . . the remaining standing black men had gotten off the bus and left the scene."[14]

Black men's reluctance to challenge police abuse was isolated neither to Montgomery nor to buses. As a child, civil rights activist Robert Williams witnessed the beating of a black woman by a police officer in his hometown of Monroe, North Carolina. More than anything else, he was horrified by the failure of black male onlookers to intervene. "The emasculated black men hung their heads in shame and hurried silently [away] from the cruelly bizarre sight," he recalled. African

American men had borne the brunt of legal and extralegal violence, as well as the racially discriminatory application of the law for generations. They also dominated the South's jail and prison population. The cumulative effect of such abuse was, as Williams recognized, to emasculate black men.[15] The southern policeman and his brutal behavior toward black men, women, and children was a cruel reminder of their inability to protect their families. Conscious of the absolute power of the police, and the dangers of challenging them in such circumstances, black men suffered the psychological torment of knowing that their intervention would likely lead to an escalation of violence. To challenge police authority was viewed as such a statement of male pride and strength precisely because it was often such a deadly act. The presence of a significant number of African American men within the crowd outside the courthouse during Rosa Parks's trial is therefore yet another example of how her arrest apparently altered black behavior toward legal authorities and politicized the community.

The same day as Parks's conviction, Martin Luther King was appointed president of the Montgomery Improvement Association. Under King's leadership, the boycott lasted just over a year before the Supreme Court ruled that the segregation of Montgomery's buses was illegal. Throughout this time, city authorities had pursued a relentless campaign of harassment and intimidation. At the front line of this struggle to preserve bus segregation were the city police. In late January, exasperated city officials had launched a campaign of arrests against boycott supporters. Car pool drivers, in particular, became police targets. On January 26, Martin Luther King was arrested for driving thirty miles per hour in a twenty-five-miles-per-hour zone. He was placed in a police car and driven to the city jail. Before nightfall, King was freed on his own recognizance. Taylor Branch, one of the few historians to examine this episode in King's life, has portrayed it as an immediate shock to King, but otherwise Branch places relatively little significance upon King's first time in jail.[16] Yet, up until this point, the role of imprisonment in nonviolent protest had not figured strongly in King's message. Days after his first jail experience, he exhorted his audience at a mass meeting to not fear imprisonment. Offering a mixture of Gandhian and Christian nonviolence, he argued that going to jail was "a very small price to pay for what we are fighting for." [17]

The city's intensification of legal repression exposed the boycott's middle-class supporters to arrest and criminal charges; this was a situation that very few had found themselves in before. Almost a month after King's first arrest, news came that a grand jury had returned indictments on 115 of Montgomery's African Americans for violating an antiboycott law. This included the MIA leadership. To date there had been relatively little debate over how to respond to arrest and imprisonment, but city authorities' decision to crush the boycott through legal action and police harassment focused attention upon the issue. Those actively involved with the boycott faced an aggressive campaign of police harassment. For Ralph Abernathy, news that his name was on the list left him "a little weak at the knees. I had never in my life been arrested, nor had any member of my family; and though we had discussed the distinct possibility that this moment might arrive, I wasn't really prepared for it." When a deputy arrived at his home, Abernathy felt the weight of his upbringing bearing down. "I could almost see my parents' scornful faces watching me, full of disapproval. I had been taught that the law was next to God in its claim on my conscience and that there was almost nothing worse than a jailbird." Abernathy's reaction was not unusual; it was a challenge to overcome the combination of fear and "terrible humiliation" at being criminalized. This was particularly the case for such middle-class men, who often perceived incarceration as a mark of the lower classes.[18]

Abernathy's fears were eased upon his arrival at the courthouse. Nixon had been the first of the indictees to arrive, and, having voluntarily submitted himself to the sheriff, he had already been booked and released on bond long before Abernathy arrived. News soon began to spread that Nixon had left the courthouse smiling. His "ordeal" now appeared to have been a lighthearted affair. As news spread, more indictees followed Nixon's example and made their own way to the courthouse. A crowd of well-wishers started to gather outside. They cheered jubilantly whenever a boycott supporter left the building.

Those able to provide the three-hundred-dollar bond were finger-printed and allowed to leave. Few people even saw the inside of a cell that day.[19] Once again, attempts to use mass arrest to isolate and intimidate key figures in the campaign had worked only to strengthen the resolve of the black community as a whole. This phase of the boycott returns us again to the politicizing impact of arrest and imprisonment upon both the individual and the wider community. The fact that the authorities had targeted members of the middle class had allowed arrest to act as a leveling factor, reducing the distance, both physically and psychologically, between working- and middle-class African Americans. Arrest and imprisonment, which had worked traditionally to suppress civil rights activity and destroy black pride, had taken on a different meaning. It is wrong to assert that this change was all-consuming; one must ask whether some individuals felt coerced into welcoming their arrest by the celebratory attitude of the black community. Furthermore, these mass arrests presented grave practical challenges to the future of the campaign. Although supporters of the boycott cheered those who confronted legal repression head-on, the idea that they should engage in noncooperation by refusing to pay bail was not present. Mounting this kind of legal defense was a challenge in itself, and increasingly drew energy, time, and funds away from the main task of maintaining the boycott.

Meanwhile, members of the Fellowship of Reconciliation watched as the protest grew. Perhaps recalling Jay Holmes Smith's search for "an American Negro Gandhi" fifteen years earlier, they observed that they may have found such an individual in Montgomery.[20] The same day as the indictment of boycott leaders, the pacifist War Resisters League (WRL) dispatched Bayard Rustin to Montgomery to assist King and the MIA in developing the nonviolent aspect of the boycott. Less than a week later, Glenn Smiley arrived to work on behalf of FOR.[21] By April the WRL reported that "the Reverend Martin Luther King, Jr. . . . is developing a decidedly Gandhi-like view. . . . He is eagerly learning all that he can about nonviolence." Smiley reported to FOR that "a full-scale revolutionary situation exists," and that he was "thrilled with the potentialities of the leadership of their youthful

Negro Gandhi."[22] References to King as a "Gandhi" figure were, however, misleading. Jay Holmes Smith and his fellow pacifists appeared to believe that if they worked hard enough at setting a nonviolent example to southern blacks, and provided them with a "Gandhi-like" leader, they would be drawn into a nonviolent uprising against segregation. Yet southern African Americans were already familiar with examples of nonviolent resistance. Boycotts and other forms of mass protest were a well-established part of southern black protest strategies. Southern black culture, dominated as it was by the black church, placed great value upon the concept of redemptive suffering. In spite of the willingness of the black community to challenge the arrests of King and other organizers, he was still a long way from being able to lead his supporters to jail. There was a yawning gap between supporting those arrested by cheering outside the courthouse and going to jail oneself. The arrests that took place during the boycott helped lessen the stigma of arrest and imprisonment, but the majority of Montgomery's African Americans were still unwilling to challenge the power of the jail cell with their own bodies.

The boycott finally came to an end in December 1956. Over the following three years, King and his newly formed organization, the Southern Christian Leadership Conference, continued to discuss how they could move beyond the lessons learned in Montgomery. While a number of nonviolent protests took place, the SCLC's early years were far from a time of innovation in civil rights protest. King and his organization remained in a nonviolent no-man's-land during the late 1950s: deeply dedicated to nonviolence, yet unsure how to secure the mass involvement of African Americans. As one historian has noted, the Montgomery Bus Boycott did not precipitate a revolution in African Americans' perception of nonviolent direct action. To refuse to ride the buses was one thing; to confront segregation openly demanded a much greater sacrifice.[23] Even if they should avoid injury, participation in protests brought the threat of arrest, imprisonment, and economic reprisals. Furthermore, the discriminatory justice system in the South meant that many African Americans had prior convictions, making arrest even more dangerous.[24]

Black activism as a whole grew in strength during the late 1950s. In response, white authorities increasingly turned to the courts to make an example of those challenging their racial supremacy. One of the most distressing cases was that of thirty-two-year-old Clyde Kennard. In 1958, having completed his second year of law school at the University of Chicago, he applied for transfer to the lily-white Mississippi Southern College in Hattiesburg, less than fifteen miles from his home. Over the following two years, Mississippi authorities employed various strategies to persuade Kennard to drop his application. When it became clear that he would persist, they turned to less covert tactics. In 1960, Kennard was convicted of receiving five bags of stolen chicken feed worth a total of twenty-five dollars and sentenced to seven years in Parchman Penitentiary. Johnny Lee Roberts, the man who testified to having stolen the feed for Kennard from his place of employment, was given a suspended sentence. It is clear now, as it was to many members of the black community then, that the power of the criminal justice system had been used to "remove" the threat of college integration. Two years later, Kennard was diagnosed as suffering from cancer. Denied medical treatment and forced to continue working, he died in July 1963.[25]

Kennard's case was yet another reminder of the criminal justice system's power to crush civil rights activism and destroy the lives of those involved. Although protesters in Montgomery and elsewhere did their best to counter such efforts, it was a difficult battle. Legal authorities invariably took the lead in this dance between segregationists and the movement; protesters were forced into a tit-for-tat approach to such repressive measures. Nevertheless, in refusing to be cowed by the power of the police, and openly celebrating those who faced criminal charges, they made a dramatic challenge to one of the most powerful forces within the Jim Crow South. It may have been a reactive process, but it served an important purpose in enabling the protest to continue. As seen in Montgomery, grassroots activism often spurred the mostly middle-class leadership to action. Such actions were rarely motivated by nonviolent philosophy, but rather by drawing upon a larger tradition of challenging definitions of "right" and "wrong" within the Jim Crow South. By celebrating those who faced criminal charges, Montgomery's black community stated that they were not the criminals in this process, but they were also not victims. Yet it must also be remembered that the legal repression faced in Montgomery was not particularly severe. Clyde Kennard's case demonstrates the range of ways that white authorities could manipulate the legal system to their ends.

By the late 1950s, Martin Luther King was calling upon activists to "take a firm and courageous stand against police brutality. We must go out and no longer be afraid to go to jail."[26] Radical pacifists were encouraged by King's developing philosophy, and continued to hope that he would fulfill their vision of him as an "American Negro Gandhi" who would lead "his" people to fill the jails. Such a hope grossly overstated the power of one person to overturn generations of legal abuse, however, while also underestimating the difficulty of such a process. King alone could never inspire a mass nonviolent movement, and he certainly could not transform attitudes toward arrest and imprisonment with mere words. This was a dynamic process, and not the product of any one individual or organization. Responses to legal harassment were shaped by the interplay between the ambitions and strategies of the movement and the responses of white authorities to protest. These factors, grounded in the specific conditions faced by activists in their own communities, were constantly changing. However, the national civil rights organizations did have their own policies regarding how activists should respond to arrest and imprisonment, and these evidently influenced the activists in individual communities. Thus, we can see that responses to arrest and imprisonment were also the product of a two-way relationship between national civil rights organizations and local campaigns.

The following chapter explores one of the most important phases in this history: the first mass imprisonment of civil rights activists. Those involved in the sit-in movement, which spread across the South during the spring of 1960, took the most radical step yet toward making the southern jail a front line in the civil rights struggle. The African American college students who dominated the sit-in protests were ready and willing to be arrested, and thousands were. Never before had the South seen its jails filled to bursting with defiant protesters. Even more importantly, they started the process of developing an ideology that embraced arrest and imprisonment as a positive experience which, when undertaken en masse, had the power to positively change race relations. It was a bold and brave move that won some victories for the movement, but often at great personal expense to those involved.

2

Jail-No-Bail!

"Now it is a nice thing to go to jail," proclaimed the *Afro-American* to its readers on March 5, 1960. The rather strange headline referred to the recent sit-in protests against lunch counter segregation, in which large numbers of students had been arrested on such charges as "trespassing" and "disorderly conduct." The "ordinary jail," the article continued, had been "transferred and changed overnight from a detention house of evil-doers into a Golgotha where innocent men are crucified for their ideas."[1] The protests had started with the now-famous sit-in at Woolworth's lunch counter in Greensboro, North Carolina, on February 1. Four black students from Greensboro Agricultural and Technical College sat down at the segregated lunch counter and requested service. Their request was denied, but they remained seated until the store closed. The following day they returned with reinforcements from campus and repeated their protest. By the end of the week, over three hundred students were taking part in the protests.[2] News of the Greensboro sit-ins soon spread to neighboring towns and states, where black college students followed their example. Over the following month, sit-in protests occurred in thirty-four cities in North Carolina, South Carolina, Virginia, Florida, Tennessee, Maryland, Kentucky, and Alabama.[3] By the time the *Afro-American* published its editorial on March 5, the number of arrests had reached 240, but rocketed over the next four weeks to above 1,000.[4]

The sheer number of arrests alone made the sit-in protests a truly revolutionary moment in the history of the southern civil rights struggle. The question of how to deal with mass arrest and imprisonment had been debated within civil rights circles for many years. Those who favored nonviolent protest knew that the nature of their response to legal repression could make the difference between success and failure. Their ideas, however, remained largely untested. This all changed with the sit-in movement. Although arrests had been made during the Montgomery and Baton Rouge bus boycotts, the number was miniscule in comparison to those made during the spring and summer of 1960. Never before had white segregationists or the movement had to contend with arrests on this scale.

Of course, this was not yet a united "movement." Rather, the individual protests were rooted in the nature of both race relations and black leadership in individual communities. Although there were pockets of protest that were clearly shaped by Gandhian philosophy, and often guided by individuals who had prior experience with such protest, these were the exception rather than the rule. Nevertheless, the black press, and the *Afro-American* in particular, tended to focus upon such examples, and disseminated the ideology behind them to a wider audience. This was particularly true when it came to responses to arrest and imprisonment. In the majority of sit-in campaigns, arrest was seen simply as a natural consequence of openly challenging racial segregation. Although protesters often celebrated those who had been arrested, they rarely sought to push this further in the early days of the sit-ins. It was only with the formation of the Student Nonviolent

Coordinating Committee in April 1960 that the concept of a Gandhian response to arrest—one which embraced imprisonment as a mark of honor, accompanied by a refusal to post bail—was brought to the fore.

In the years before the Greensboro four chose to make their protest, southern black college students were already experimenting with the sit-in tactic. In the winter of 1959, the Nonviolent Action Group from Howard University sat in at a lunch counter in Arlington, Virginia. The students were beaten by onlookers and subsequently arrested. In 1959, John Brown was dispatched to Miami, Florida, on behalf of CORE to coordinate sit-in protests. A series of protests took place against segregated lunch counters during the spring and summer. Following the beating of protesters, CORE counseled Brown to avoid arrests, fearing the disruptive impact this might have upon the growing level of support they were receiving. In Durham, North Carolina, an ice cream parlor had been the focus of a series of sit-in protests during the late 1950s. Those involved had been arrested, and faced a lengthy court battle.[5] It is far from clear why these earlier protests did not spark the same reaction as the Greensboro sit-ins. Miles Wolff has pointed to the moderate nature of Greensboro race relations; it was a city "conscious of its image and unwilling to have the students arrested or inflict violence on them."[6] Certainly, Greensboro authorities reacted to the sit-ins in a more restrained manner than did those at the locations of many of the earlier protests. Furthermore, as William Chafe has demonstrated, the sit-ins were part of a much longer protest tradition within Greensboro's black community. The sit-ins "represented a dramatic extension of, rather than a departure from, traditional patterns of black activism in Greensboro."[7]

The rising number of arrests during the spring of 1960 reflected the way in which segregationists in many communities responded to sit-in protests with a determined campaign of legal harassment. Their intention was clear: they wanted to force the students to abandon their campaigns against lunch counter segregation. George Lewis's work on the segregationist response to the civil rights movement makes it clear that white authorities were confronted with a new challenge during and after the sit-ins. Segregationists lost the initiative from 1960 as protests expanded and became ever more confrontational. The sit-in protests, closely followed by a number of other nonviolent campaigns, brought the battle between the civil rights movement and segregationists onto the streets, onto the buses, and into stores such as Woolworth's. Such a "theatrical" way of demonstrating the inequalities of southern society made segregation both a very real and a highly emotive issue. As Lewis shows, it became much harder for segregationists to argue that southern blacks were content with their lot.[8] While this confrontational approach clearly helped the civil rights movement in one sense, it also intensified other challenges and problems. Most importantly for the purposes of this study, it increased the movement's vulnerability to legal repression. The response of segregationists at the state level was invariably to turn to the law. State legislatures shored up the power of legal authorities to prosecute protesters by passing a raft of new laws and creating investigative committees. For example, the Georgia legislature passed a new anti-trespass law making far more severe penalties available to the courts. Louisiana followed a similar path: laws against disorderly conduct, criminal mischief, and trespass were revised to allow for more punitive sentences. The crime of disturbing the peace now included those acts which "did, or might 'forseeably,' disturb or alarm the public." These measures were clearly aimed at sit-in protesters.[9] At the local level, police authorities were more than ready to use their new powers. Legal repression became one of the most important weapons that white authorities deployed against protesters. It was not a new way of suppressing protest, but the manner of nonviolent protests that took place during the 1960s made it a far more important tool for segregationists.

As the Greensboro sit-ins continued, students in other southern towns and cities instigated their own campaigns to desegregate lunch counters. On February 8, students in both Durham and Winston-Salem, North Carolina, became the first to follow the example of the Greensboro four and started sit-ins at segregated lunch counters. By the end of February, sit-ins had taken place in at least thirty towns and cities across North Carolina and Virginia, and had reached into communities as far south as Florida and Alabama.[10]

In Raleigh, North Carolina, the first arrests of the sit-in movement were made on February 12. At the request of a local businessman, police escorted forty-three demonstrators to jail. Upon hearing of the initial arrests more students joined the protests, ready to go to jail. While the students were willing to submit to imprisonment, they were not convinced of the value of remaining there. They were quickly released on fifty-dollar bonds.[11]

Shortly after these arrests, Martin Luther King traveled to nearby Durham at the request of Douglas Moore, a minister and SCLC member. Before speaking at a rally at White Rock Baptist Church, King met with a delegation of local student activists to discuss nonviolent techniques. When discussion moved to the question of arrest, King issued a warning to the students: "If there's any mistake made by us in Montgomery, it was that we were too anxious to avoid jail when arrested. There is a strong redemptive value in unmerited suffering." Whether inspired by recent events in Raleigh or by King's appeal, a number within the group came to an agreement: if arrested, they would refuse bail.[12] At a rally later that evening, King returned to the question of imprisonment, offering one of the strongest expositions yet on the need to reject bail. Their struggle, he told the audience, was not "between white and black people," but between "justice and injustice." Warning that they were "in for a season of suffering," he implored those around him to "not fear going to jail. If the officials threaten to arrest us for standing up for our rights, we must answer by saying that we are willing and prepared to fill up the jails of the South."[13] Some at the time may have observed that, so far, King had hardly followed his own advice. His failure to secure a jail term as evidence of his commitment to nonviolence was perhaps both a frustration and a relief to King. Yet, if King was reluctant to commit to a jail term, he was clearly not alone.

During February and March 1960, over one thousand sit-in protesters were arrested in towns and cities across the South. As Aldon Morris has demonstrated, networks of experienced nonviolent activists provided support and training to the students. Men such as James McCain, Floyd McKissick, and Reverend C. K. Steele were well-versed in nonviolent philosophy, including the rejection of bail. Yet the vast majority of students chose to accept bail, and most were quickly released.[14] In the majority of cases, students had reconciled themselves to the possibility of imprisonment long before they openly challenged the segregation laws. A commitment to going to jail, however, was very different from *remaining* in jail voluntarily. As Adam Fairclough has observed, there was significant opposition among communities to moving beyond boycotts toward more confrontational forms of nonviolence where arrest and imprisonment became a far greater threat.[15] The conservatism of black communities often placed pressure on students to limit their protests. While some adults may have been able to accept the decision to risk imprisonment, the concept that students would accept criminal charges without challenge was clearly more problematic. Simultaneously, many students themselves held conservative values. Sit-in participants tended to stress their conservative, middle-class aims: becoming a "criminal" did not sit well with these values.[16] Perhaps most important of all is the fact that nobody could be sure how local police would react to these mass protests. To remain in jail—one of the most dangerous places to be under such circumstances—was not a common decision. Yet attitudes toward arrest and imprisonment were clearly changing, and most noticeably among students. At the same time that protesters were leaving jail, many were also expressing faith in the power of unjust imprisonment as a force for change. Student after student testified to the way in which the simple act of being arrested had renewed their determination to fight racial injustice. "This experience of being jailed has made us even more determined than we were at first," claimed the leader of the Winston-Salem sit-in protests, Carl Matthews. "We are not going to cease for one minute—we'll be even more forceful than before."[17] While they may not have spent much time behind bars, this was truly an example of imprisonment politicizing the prisoner.[18] Within a matter of months, a consensus had emerged among the nascent student movement that the celebration of imprisonment as a mark of honor and a positive experience should figure centrally in their protest ideology.

The *Afro-American* carried numerous articles and editorials on the students' sacrifice. Alongside the headline stating "Now It Is A Nice Thing To Go To Jail" were others declaring jail "A Weapon For The Strong and Brave" and "It's Worth Going To Jail For." The March 5 edition included a number of articles on the arrested students, and went to great lengths to explain why the students now felt that "it is a nice thing to go to jail." "It would appear," the article concluded, "there is no freedom for the humble, the disadvantaged and the exploited, unless they have served a term in jail because there is no such thing as winning freedom without voluntary sacrifices."[19] Black newspapers such as the *Afro-American* helped spread the idea of imprisonment as a positive and liberating experience during the spring of 1960. At the heart of such rhetoric lay an attempt to transform the jail from a symbol of white power and a site of black repression into a symbol of black protest and a site of black empowerment. Central to this transformation was the evolution of an ideology that embraced "freedom" as a critical rhetorical component. As Richard King has observed, the idea of freedom was so influential within the movement because it could be won by African Americans, rather than granted to them (as was the case with "civil rights"). Freedom was a state of mind, and something that could be achieved in both an individual and collective sense. It is clear that changing attitudes toward arrest and imprisonment plugged into this wider emphasis upon freedom. By *choosing* to go to jail, movement participants placed an emphasis upon securing one's mental freedom from fear, even at the cost of one's physical freedom. In this context, it is possible to appreciate how such a redefinition of jail was central to the overall effectiveness of the nonviolent movement. Given that the police, courts, and jails were the principle guardians of the Jim Crow South, the movement had to help African Americans overcome their fear of arrest and imprisonment. Indeed, this fits nicely with Richard King's argument that historians need to look beyond the role of freedom as a static concept within the movement, and instead explore how it was *experienced* within the movement.[20] The jail experience is the most important example of how the idea of freedom was deployed by the movement; and—to return to the *Afro-American*—the black press was a crucial vehicle for communicating this transformation.

The sit-in movement reached Orangeburg, South Carolina, in late February. Students at local Claflin College had organized a chapter of the NAACP in the early 1950s. The chapter grew stronger in the wake of the *Brown v. Board of Education* decision, helping to organize a boycott of local businesses after the White Citizens Council targeted supporters of school desegregation for economic reprisals.[21] The Congress of Racial Equality's James McCain, who had spent most of February traveling through the state training students in nonviolence, arrived in Orangeburg late in the month. He spent a short time with the students advising them on how to start their own protests, then moved on to speak to students in Durham, North Carolina. Shortly after, on February 25, forty-five students staged the city's first sit-in.[22] The following day, sixty students from both Claflin and South Carolina State College staged a second sit-in, where there was a single arrest. From then on, support for protests grew with astonishing speed. A mass march through the streets of Orangeburg less than a week later attracted eleven hundred participants. As was the case in a number of other towns and cities, legal authorities assumed a largely neutral position. While racial customs dictated that such a challenge to the color line should be met with strict punishment, police forces were often unsure about how to react and were generally reluctant to fill their jails with hundreds of students. This early reticence to punish (which must have emboldened the protesters) soon disappeared. Two weeks after the first mass march, more than a thousand students again met to march upon Memorial Plaza, the central city square. The police, however, had clearly changed tactics: the students were subjected to a barrage of tear gas, while the fire department turned water hoses upon them. At least fifty of the marchers required medical attention. One female student suffered injuries to her eyes; another lost three teeth. At one point, a hose was trained upon a student who had already been knocked down by the water pressure. She was later hospitalized with a fractured knee. By the time the tear gas had cleared, a total of 388 students had been taken into custody. Clearly, the "honeymoon" period between the police and protesters had passed.[23] The Orangeburg jail, with a maximum capacity of fifty-eight, was soon overflowing. The majority of the students were forced into an open stockade without shelter from the ravages of the cold March weather. A suspected leader of the protest, Isaac Arnold, was locked in the hole: a "damp, dungeon-like cell" with water covering the floor, which prisoners were placed in as a form of punishment. The ordeal left Arnold suffering from exposure.[24] Many members of the local black community immediately rallied to support the students. Mrs. Helen Thompson, owner of a local soda shop, provided food to the prisoners. Local businessmen furnished the ten-dollar-per-person bail, which the students readily accepted. Upon their release, the president of Claflin College, Dr. H. Manning, provided the students with a hot meal.[25] This was by far the most extreme example of police brutality against protesters to date. The NAACP was shocked by the viciousness of the police attack upon its members. Shortly after the students' release, NAACP national youth secretary Herbert Wright traveled to Claflin College to congratulate the students on their nonviolent protest and encourage them to continue. Meanwhile, news of the events had spread far and wide. A large photograph of students in the stockade, and accompanying details of their treatment, dominated the front page of the *New York Times* the next day. The Orangeburg arrests indicated the extent to which mass arrests accompanied by police brutality could attract mainstream media interest.[26]

Of all the sit-in movements that emerged during the spring of 1960, none played a more important role in shaping the future ideology and direction of the civil rights movement's responses to mass arrest and imprisonment than the one in Nashville, Tennessee. It was in Nashville that students first rejected bail, and the group quickly became the strongest advocates of what they came to call "jail-no-bail." Students in Nashville, as in other towns and cities, had been discussing and experimenting with nonviolence long before the Greensboro protest ignited student discontent. Critically, they benefited from the counsel of James Lawson, who was a devoted and knowledgeable proponent of nonviolent direct action. Lawson had been imprisoned as a conscientious objector for a year after he refused to serve in the Korean War. Subsequently he worked as a missionary in India and as southern field secretary for the Fellowship of Reconciliation. Like many radical pacifists, Lawson was eager to challenge segregation through nonviolent direct action, including the rejection of bail. When he registered as a theology student at Vanderbilt University in Nashville in 1959, Lawson immediately set about organizing workshops on nonviolence. The group Lawson organized had experimented with sit-ins in late 1959. By February 1960, the group working with Lawson was already well schooled in nonviolence. Sit-ins started in Nashville on February 13. After observing the protests for a full week, the police finally responded to the students' challenge by arresting protesters at McClellan's store.[27] For the Nashville students, the simple experience of *challenging* white authority, being *jailed,* and *surviving* was deeply empowering. John Lewis, one of the arrested students, recalled:

> It was strange how I felt as a large, blue-shirted Nashville police officer stood over me and said without emotion, "You're under arrest." A lifetime of taboos from my parents rushed through my mind as the officer gripped me by the bicep of my left arm. *Don't get in trouble. Stay away from Love Street. Only bad people go to jail.*
>
> I could see my mother's face now. I could hear her voice: *Shameful. Disgraceful.*[28]

To go to jail not only brought the threat of family disapproval, it also forced protesters to confront the fear of imprisonment that a century of violence and discrimination had ingrained into many African Americans' minds. For so long, a key element of the threat of jail was the fear that one would be forgotten, ignored, and left at the complete mercy of the authorities. During 1960, the majority of protesters were imprisoned en masse, something which greatly helped individuals overcome this fear. "When we got to the city jail, the place was awash with a sense of jubilation," remembered Lewis. "With all these friends, these familiar faces piling out of those wagons, it felt like a crusade, as if we were prisoners in a holy war."[29] These early arrests helped to alleviate much of the stress of the experience by creating a sense of community among the protesters. As many were imprisoned for only a short period of time, this exuberant atmosphere was not destroyed by division over tactics and leadership. The Nashville students were the first to embrace jail-no-bail as part of their nonviolent movement. "We were happy to be in jail for this cause," recalls Lewis. "We were not about to cooperate in any way with a system that allowed the discrimination we were protesting. . . . We sang, and we chanted: 'Jail without bail!'"[30] Unsure how to respond to such a challenge, police released the protesters after only six hours.

While the Nashville students were filling the jails, members of the CORE chapter in Tallahassee, Florida, were also experimenting with the rejection of bail. The Tallahassee chapter, which operated out of the local NAACP office, had been organized by local students in October 1959. Congress of Racial Equality members had already tested segregation on buses and held a sit-in at a downtown department store with little reaction from the white community. As in Nashville, news of the Greensboro protests inspired a renewed protest campaign. On February 20, less than a week after the start of the campaign and much to the surprise of CORE, a sit-in protest ended in the arrest of all eleven participants.[31] The imprisonment of the protesters appears to have shaken the CORE membership, which acted nervously in the face of arrest. White members of CORE—which comprised around sixty percent of the membership—were warned to stay away from the NAACP office for fear that their presence might incite violence. Plans for sit-ins over the next two weeks were cancelled in the belief that such protest could "hasten the trial date."[32] Further protests did not take place until March 12, when integrated groups of students descended upon the lunch counters at Woolworth's and McCrory's. The protest in McCrory's ended when the lunch counter was closed, but in Woolworth's the six students were arrested. One CORE member rushed to the Florida Agricultural and Mechanical University (FAMU) campus and called upon her fellow students to "march on Woolworth's and McCrory's" and "fill the jails if necessary." One hundred students responded to her pleas and marched on

McCrory's store, where twenty were arrested. Determined to continue their protest, the remaining students left McCrory's and headed toward Woolworth's, only to find their path blocked by a group of angry whites. Their plans frustrated, the group returned to campus, where news of the intimidation inspired around one thousand students to march again upon Woolworth's. This time the protesters were intercepted not by white youths, but by the Tallahassee police. Verdine Smith, who participated in the march that day, described how "The policemen started toward us in a skirmish line formation. They threw tear gas grenades at us. . . . I was momentarily blinded. When I looked around again, I saw officers trying to circle us." Smith, along with many other members of the march, was taken to the county jail and subsequently charged with disorderly conduct. After two days, he was one of the last to be released when his father posted a five-hundred-dollar bond. The attack upon the marchers by police, which paralleled that in Orangeburg, resulted in another temporary suspension of demonstrations.[33]

The eleven arrested in the February Tallahassee sit-ins came to trial the same week as the police attack upon the marchers from FAMU. They were charged with a bewildering array of offenses in an apparent attempt to ensure that none escaped conviction. Once in court, most of these charges were dropped; however, all were found guilty of disturbing the peace and inciting a riot. Faced with a sixty-day sentence or a three-hundred-dollar fine, eight chose to remain in jail. In contrast to those in Nashville, who were bailed out of jail shortly, this constituted an outright refusal to cooperate with legal authorities.[34] The group's spokesperson was student Patricia Stephens. In a letter from jail to James Robinson of CORE, she explained their decision to reject bail by referring to King's meeting with students in Raleigh. "We strongly believe that Martin Luther King was right," she wrote, "when he said 'we've got to fill the jails in order to win our equal rights.'"[35] The eight attracted considerable attention from CORE. Having struggled to make a mark on the South since the late 1950s, events in Tallahassee appeared to confirm that the organization's influence was growing.

The students' example also made an impact outside of CORE. The fact that one of the eight was the sixteen-year-old son of C. K. Steele, the SCLC's vice president, gave that organization an indirect influence over events. In a letter of support sent to the students, King praised their actions, defining their imprisonment as a "badge of honor."[36] A. J. Muste of the Fellowship of Reconciliation also wrote to the jailed students, congratulating them for their determined stance: "I am a kind of grandfather of CORE, I suppose, and I certainly have never experienced a deeper emotional satisfaction about any share I may have had in its work greater than your action and your statement about it have given me. It is seldom that one's actions and one's words about it are in such complete accord."[37]

For Patricia Stephens's parents, her jailing, along with that of her sister Priscilla, was hard to accept. After twenty-four hours they arrived at the jail ready to remove their daughters; the sisters persuaded them otherwise. According to Patricia Stephens's letters, their time in jail was relatively tolerable. On April 17, Easter Sunday, the jailer allowed them to leave the visiting room with friends and family to spend time together in the grounds. "We all got acquainted," described Stephens, "and hid easter eggs . . . and also took pictures." Later, the sisters were again allowed out of jail to spend time with their grandmother, who was too frail to leave the family car.[38] The brutality used against protesters by police during the march on Woolworth's does not appear to have continued behind bars. Any stay in jail, with the associated lack of privacy, comfort, and decent food, was stressful and demanding for civil rights workers; nevertheless, on this occasion the eight prisoners appear to have escaped the type of physical and psychological abuse suffered by those in Orangeburg.

On April 1, students from across the South arrived at Shaw University in Raleigh, North Carolina, to share their experiences and discuss the future of the nonviolent movement. They did so amid a worsening legal situation. Over the preceding two months, southern courts had been awash with sit-in protesters. Never before had the region had to contend with such a challenge to its Jim Crow laws. In the upper South, some white communities desegregated eating facilities with remarkable speed. Elsewhere, authorities resorted to a dual-pronged attack of official violence combined with mass arrest. In Tallahassee and Orangeburg there was a clear lag between the start of arrests and the eventual use of violent force and mass arrest. In much of the Deep South that gap was far shorter.

By the time of the Shaw Conference, the NAACP reported that over one thousand students had been arrested as part of the sit-in movement. Unsurprisingly, the need to formulate a clear and coherent response to arrest was a central point of discussion at the Shaw University meeting. Martin Luther King opened the conference by presenting a series of recommendations, including the need to create a cohort of volunteers dedicated to spending time in jail. James Lawson similarly emphasized the importance of rejecting bail as part of a nonviolent philosophy, something the Nashville group was distinguished by. Charles McDew, who had emerged as a local leader of the Orangeburg protests and was present at the conference, recalled: "there were these very eloquent people from Nashville who understood the philosophy, who understood the reason behind it . . . we knew in Orangeburg that we had been doing this nonviolent direct action strictly as a tactic and we learned so much."[39] It was at the Shaw Conference that many students who had previously accepted bail learned the rationale for remaining in jail from the Nashville contingent.[40]

Future meetings of SNCC underlined the importance of jail-no-bail. In May, CORE's Len Holt called upon activists to "depend less on appeals to the courts and more on appeals to conscience. If we go to jail by the hundreds and thousands, the hearts of those who would maintain the old order will be inundated with the guilt necessary to bring about change."[41] The same month, Lawson urged SNCC to demonstrate its commitment to jail-no-bail. He explained, "we lost the finest hour of this movement when so many of us left the jails across the South. Instead of letting the adults scurry around getting bail, we should have insisted that they scurry about to end the system that put us in jail. If history offers us such an opportunity again, let us be prepared to seize it."[42] James Lawson and Len Holt, as radical pacifists with experience following their own advice, were acutely aware that the way in which people responded to imprisonment could make or break the nascent movement, and worked hard to convince individuals and organizations of the importance of refusing bail.

The jail-no-bail rhetoric heralded the jail experience playing a pivotal role in liberating African Americans from the psychological controls of white supremacy. Adopting a positive view of the jail experience was crucial to the ongoing popularity of nonviolent protest, and it is evident from the testimony of many of those involved in the sit-ins that imprisonment was a truly transformative experience. Less understood, however, are those individuals who did not experience this transformation. Julian Bond, one of the foremost organizers in the Atlanta sit-in movement, chose not to return to jail after his first arrest. "I wasn't interested in doing it again . . . [there was] no brutality or unpleasantness at all. . . . It was just an experience I didn't want to go through again." The degree to which some members of the movement, particularly in SNCC, saw imprisonment as a "badge of honor" brought the danger of portraying those who chose not to go to jail as somehow less honorable. Whether or not others viewed Julian Bond in this light, he was fully aware of the conflict himself. "Other members of the movement were arrested five, 10, I think some as many as 15 times on different occasions. But I consciously avoided it and felt quite guilty about it then, and feel quite guilty about it now."[43] Bond's openness on this subject, recorded in a 1968 interview, offers an alternative view of imprisonment. Evidence of this sentiment being more widespread in the movement is hard to come by, yet it seems logical that acceptance of the "positive" nature of imprisonment was not monolithic. Indeed, arrest and imprisonment was not a ubiquitous experience among civil rights activists. Many individuals committed their lives to the struggle but nonetheless felt that they could not risk imprisonment. Financial or family commitments could act as strong deterrents to being arrested. For example, a single mother, no matter how committed to the movement, could not realistically consider spending an untold length of time in jail. Such people often chose to undertake roles which were absolutely crucial to the movement's survival, but which were less likely to attract the attention of the police.

As the oldest and most experienced nonviolent civil rights organization, CORE was sensitive to the possibility that jail-no-bail could assume a coercive dimension. A CORE memorandum by Executive Secretary James Robinson, apparently written during the summer of 1960, reveals a somewhat more pragmatic take than SNCC's on the problems posed by mass arrest and imprisonment of civil rights protesters. Robinson felt it necessary to caution against pressuring people to go to jail, and warned that jail-no-bail was not always desirable: "The decision to stay in jail . . . should be left up to the individual. . . . Also, organizations . . . should not push the value of jail without giving the individual an out. Certainly, going to jail for some is relatively easy and for others very difficult indeed."[44] This was by far one of the most sophisticated analyses of the implications of jail-no-bail, and it foresaw some of the challenges that CORE, SNCC, and the SCLC would face in future campaigns.

For the NAACP, the question of whether to reject bail was deeply problematic and brought into sharp contrast the philosophical differences between itself, SNCC, SCLC, and CORE. Established in 1909 as a biracial organization, the NAACP had, more than any other group, seen firsthand the horrific conditions and treatment meted out to black prisoners in the South. Deeply aware that the southern criminal justice system was one of the key ways by which southern white communities controlled the lives of African Americans, the NAACP dedicated significant resources to challenging the operation of this system. From the very beginning, therefore, the organization had both practical and philosophical objections to jail-no-bail. The NAACP had been at the forefront of defending African Americans from this brutality and injustices of southern jails and prisons for half a century. As a national civil rights organization, it struggled to appreciate that imprisonment could be anything other than a social stigma. During the early months of the sit-ins, both the NAACP National Office and the Legal Defense Fund played a crucial role in performing the mammoth task of raising bail money and defending protesters in the courts.[45] Within six weeks of the Greensboro sit-in, the NAACP had raised forty thousand dollars and enlisted fifty lawyers to defend over one thousand protesters in court.[46] Thurgood Marshall, head of the Legal Defense Fund, publicly pledged that his organization would appeal every conviction, regardless of the cost—although one cannot help but feel that he may not have fully anticipated just how many arrests would take place.[47] Despite this commitment to supporting arrested protesters, there were signs of division over tactics almost from the beginning. While pledging the support of the Fund, Marshall commented, "Those boys and girls didn't check the law when they sat down on those stools. . . . Now we're going to have to check the law."[48] This feeling of bitterness—that they had somehow been cajoled into defending the students—would intensify over the following years.

Despite a considerable commitment within SNCC, SCLC, and CORE to fill the jails, the example set by the Tallahassee and Nashville students remained exceptional during 1960. Although there had been a large number of arrests during the first months of sit-ins, few students welcomed the idea of forfeiting bail. For the NAACP, this general willingness to accept bail enabled them to remain supportive of the student movement. During April and May, however, appeals for people to reject bail intensified and the national office found it increasingly difficult to accept the actions of arrested protesters. In a discussion on jail-no-bail with Ella Baker, Thurgood Marshall made it quite clear that, as a lawyer, he deeply disapproved of anyone refusing bail, and that he would most likely refuse to accept any such case.[49] This statement must have served only to confirm the feeling among younger, militant activists that the NAACP was out of touch with the current mood of civil rights protest. This sentiment was expressed most clearly by James Lawson at the Shaw University Conference, when he attacked the NAACP as a "black bourgeois club" and "a fund-raising agency," while also calling for an elite corps of volunteers dedicated to remaining in jail. Roy Wilkins issued a threat to cut off all relations with SCLC unless Lawson was removed from the organization.[50] King, keen to maintain a working relationship with the NAACP, accepted Lawson's resignation.

In excess of fifteen hundred protesters were arrested as part of the sit-in movement. While the *Afro-American*'s claim that it was "a nice thing to go to jail" was apocryphal, many found their time in jail to be a liberating and politicizing experience.[51] Passing through the jailhouse door had become a form of induction into the movement. If some individuals celebrated going to jail as part of their commitment to Gandhian nonviolence, it was not just nonviolent ideology that motivated such a response. Perhaps of even greater importance was the celebration of imprisonment as an honorable act. By doing this, the movement helped overcome the fear of jail and shame associated with gaining a criminal record. Nevertheless, not everybody wanted to or could go to jail. Despite the loud calls for jail-no-bail, only a small number of protesters remained incarcerated for any length of time.[52] Even in Tallahassee, local leaders complained that supporters quickly requested they be released on bail. Furthermore, the majority of protesters were unwilling to accept criminal charges without a fight. When the courts had done so much to nurture and sustain the Jim Crow system, it did not make sense to sit in jail without challenging those courts. It is here that the NAACP and the Legal Defense Fund served a crucial role. Local lawyers who were willing to take on civil rights cases were few and far between, and SNCC could not sustain the economic costs of challenging convictions. Without the aid of the NAACP and Defense Fund's lawyers and bail fund, sit-in protesters would have faced a far bleaker legal situation. The adoption of jail-no-bail and the celebration of the jail experience, therefore, was not as great a leap from the NAACP's legalistic approach to challenging racism as was suggested by the newspaper's headlines. It was partly a response to the historic abuse of African Americans by police, courts, and jailers, and although some protesters refused to cooperate with the legal system in any way, far more refused to be criminalized by immoral and unjust laws. However, in the immediate aftermath of the sit-ins, activists questioned whether their readiness to accept bail had undermined the effectiveness of their protests. As the following chapter reflects, the experience of arrest and imprisonment during the sit-ins, as well as the vibrant debate over how best to respond to such repression, brought about a deepening commitment within SNCC, SCLC, and CORE to exploiting mass imprisonment as *both* a moral and strategic challenge to the Jim Crow South. Drawing upon a belief that the key to destroying the Jim Crow South lay within the jail cell, civil rights activists would place the tactic of mass imprisonment at the forefront of the movement the following year.

3

From Sit-Ins to Jail-Ins

By the fall of 1960, the civil rights movement as a whole had *talked* at length about filling the jails, but very few individuals had actually served a full jail sentence. With a malaise upon the sit-in movement, "jail-in" became the new buzzword for 1961. In addition to a refusal to accept bail, jail-ins sought to place moral and financial pressure upon southern authorities by filling the jails with protesters for prolonged periods of time. This chapter explores a period in civil rights history when the use of arrest and imprisonment as a protest strategy was at its height and, in doing so, it reveals the way in which these protests, in particular the 1961 Freedom Ride, brought far longer periods of incarceration than had been typical during the sit-in protests, as well as a more diverse group of civil rights prisoners. The consequences of this development were manifold but, most importantly, it brought activists into much closer contact with the rest of the jail population. In addition to exploring these interactions, and other aspects of the activists' jail experiences, this chapter brings into view the interplay between efforts to place moral, political, and financial pressure upon white authorities, and the corresponding pressure that placed upon civil rights organizations. These jail-ins brought benefits to the movement, but they also placed civil rights organizations under massive financial and legal pressures. This chapter also highlights divisions created by the strategy of filling the jails, most especially in relations with the NAACP.

During 1961, filling the jails as a form of resistance in its own right was viewed as a radical and innovative form of protest. At the forefront of these developments was CORE, which sought to build upon its radical pacifist origins by standing at the helm of this new and exciting strategy. Besides a deep faith in Gandhian philosophy, CORE's enthusiasm for mass imprisonment was spurred on by its competition with other civil rights organizations. The Congress of Racial Equality was deeply conscious of the competition it faced from SCLC and SNCC. Lacking the charismatic leadership of King and unable to display the same militant energies of SNCC, CORE viewed leadership of a massive jail-in campaign as an opportunity to stand out from the pack.

In August 1960, CORE sponsored the second Miami Action Institute, which attracted a large number of southern college students. At the top of the discussion agenda was the jail-in. In many respects, the Institute was a great success for CORE. Not only was it able to attract a number of talented students into its fold, but James Robinson also led eighteen of those at the Institute in a lunch counter sit-in, at which they were arrested. Keen to put their discussions into practice, seven of the protesters remained in jail for the ten days prior to their trial, at which they were given suspended sentences. According to August Meier and Elliott Rudwick, CORE used its success in Miami to project an image of the organization sitting on the front line of new developments in nonviolent protest.[1]

South Carolina was one of the few southern states in which CORE had succeeded in establishing a strong presence; it was therefore a logical choice for the organization to test jail-ins. South Carolina was also home to Tom Gaither and James McCain—both strong supporters of the jail-in. Tom Gaither had been one of hundreds of students imprisoned in the Orangeburg City Jail on March 15 after police attacked protesters with fire hoses and tear gas. He had emerged from Orangeburg with a reputation as a talented leader, and CORE had quickly recruited him. Having been imprisoned as part of the Miami jail-in, he returned to his home state in December 1960 with the aim of expanding student support for mass arrests and long-term imprisonment. That month Gaither organized a CORE-sponsored student workshop in Orangeburg. Participants discussed at length the importance of remaining faithful to Gandhian philosophy when imprisoned, as well as the power of mass imprisonment to bring long-lasting change to the South.[2]

Early in 1961, Gaither sought to bring these ideas to life. He traveled to Rock Hill, a town close to Orangeburg, where there had been a determined sit-in campaign by students at Friendship Junior College. On January 31 he led a sit-in protest at McCrory's lunch counter. Almost immediately, the ten activists were arrested and subsequently convicted of trespassing. They were sentenced to a one-hundred-dollar fine or thirty days' hard labor on the road gang. One student accepted bail as the basis of a legal test case, while the remaining nine chose the road gang. "Surprise and shock filled the courtroom when it became known that we had chosen to be jailed-in," Gaither later commented. "The only thing they had to beat us over the head with was a threat of sending us to jail. So we disarmed them by using the only weapon we had left . . . jail without bail. . . . It upset them considerably."[3] All nine were black men, and accordingly were placed in the appropriate segregated section of the York County road gang stockade. Dressed in chain gang uniforms, the men were set to work loading sand onto a truck in freezing weather. As Gaither later recalled in his pamphlet "Jailed-in," black prisoners reacted to their arrival with the warning "the stuff is on!" "By the 'stuff' they meant anti-Negro hatred," Gaither later wrote. "They explained that the 'stuff' had been 'on' only recently in the white dormitory, following the much-publicized marriage of the Negro singer-actor, Sammy Davis Jr., and the white screen star, May Britt." In the highly racialized environment of the southern jail, any affront to white supremacy risked violence. The Rock Hill protesters faced a dangerous thirty days.[4] Accounts of imprisonment from 1960 generally offer little description of relations with "ordinary" prisoners. The city and county jails to which sit-in protesters were sent were often small and generally held only those awaiting trial or convicted of misdemeanor crimes. Given the speed with which many civil rights prisoners passed through the system—sometimes only spending a few hours in jail before being bailed out—there were presumably few opportunities for contact with other prisoners. Aside from the protest in Tallahassee, the Rock Hill nine were the first to serve a significant length of time alongside the general inmate population. Despite fears of racial violence, Gaither reported only one incident of direct confrontation, when a white prisoner drew a knife on two of the men.[5]

Meanwhile, the national CORE office was keen to publicize events in Rock Hill. Conscious that nine prisoners hardly amounted to "filling the jails," CORE appealed for support. Having committed itself to jail-no-bail, SNCC so far had not had the opportunity to test these values. The executive secretary, Edward King, responded to the appeal by calling for people to "join [the activists] at the lunch counters and in jail. Only by this type of action can we show that the nonviolent movement against segregation is not a local issue for just the individual community, but rather a united movement of all those who believe in equality."[6] In early February, SNCC members Charles Jones, Charles Sherrod, Ruby Doris Smith, and Diane Nash traveled to Rock Hill, and shortly after were arrested during a lunch counter sit-in. Jones and Sherrod were sentenced to thirty days' hard labor. Nash and Smith were sent to the women's section of the county jail.

The same day that the SNCC members arrived in Rock Hill, the original "jail-inners" were placed in one cramped solitary confinement cell after they refused to stop singing freedom songs. After a few hours they were returned to the road gang to load topsoil onto trucks, but the nine soon realized that they were being forced to assume a disproportionate workload. Gaither observed that the officials' strategy was to "work the hell" out of the protesters. When the grueling workload left two of them sick and injured, they responded to their treatment with a "slow-down."[7]

The Rock Hill jail-in never increased its numbers beyond the thirteen SNCC and CORE members, and all were released after their thirty-day sentences expired. The jail-in came to an end. Nevertheless, Rock Hill was celebrated within SNCC and CORE as a moral victory marking a defining moment in their commitment to nonviolence. In a more general sense, however, the campaign brought few tangible gains. Rock Hill remained as segregated as before their imprisonment. Furthermore, Gaither had hoped that the protest would become the nucleus of a massive statewide jail-in campaign. While his pamphlet claims that almost one hundred jail-ins took place across the South during February, this appears to have been an exaggeration. There was clear support for their actions, but it was not the beginning of a revolution in civil rights strategy.

One place that Rock Hill did have an impact was Atlanta. Students at Spelman College, who were loosely affiliated with SNCC, were inspired to organize their own jail-in. The intention of the predominantly female organizers was to have so many arrests that there would be no students to attend the homecoming. Despite objections from the Spelman faculty that jail was no place for women, the protests went ahead. By the second day, February 10, seventy-six protesters had been imprisoned in Fulton County Jail. After a week, Adelaide Taitte received a letter from Ruby Doris Smith and Diane Nash, who were now imprisoned as part of the Rock Hill jail-in. Given the actual conditions in Rock Hill, Smith's description of jail life is an incredible affirmation of her commitment to nonviolence. "We receive letters from all over the country congratulating us for our courageous action. I feel so guilty and unworthy because we are really enjoying ourselves. This isn't prison, it's paradise." News of life on the South Carolina road gang apparently made the Atlanta students appreciate the relative comfort of their jail cells. In a show of solidarity, the two groups of students agreed to sing "We Shall Overcome" at noon every day.[8] Just like Rock Hill, the Atlanta jail-in did not bring any tangible changes to the racial status quo. Nevertheless, those who participated gained a renewed faith in the importance of rejecting bail. Adelaide Taitt recalled that protesters left jail feeling "like a large family bound together with faith, hope, and love." "You get ideas in jail," Charles Sherrod noted. "You talk with other young people you've never seen. . . . We're up all night, sharing creativity, planning action. You learn the truth in prison, you learn wholeness. You find out the difference between being dead and alive."[9]

Talk of jail-ins and the ongoing arrest of protesters left the NAACP struggling to bridge the growing gulf between itself and the proponents of mass direct action. In February 1961, the organization finally sought to establish a policy on how members should respond to arrest. The NAACP would continue with its policy "of defending . . . persons against prosecution and . . . supplying . . . bail while their cases were . . . on appeal." Thus, while reiterating its support of "sit-ins, sit-downs, stand-ins and all other forms of youth protests," NAACP members were instructed to "plead not guilty to [any] charges and accept bail." In contrast to SNCC, CORE, and SCLC, the NAACP not only urged "bail not jail," but it also proposed that remaining in jail could be harmful to the freedom struggle: "there is a grave danger that the individual, by his failure . . . to fight a criminal charge levied against him . . . will . . . render ineffectual our overall legal attack upon this spiteful, vicious system." It was also noted that accepting bail constituted the only way to "avoid stigmatizing our youth with criminal records, the efficacy of which is extremely doubtful."[10] The memorandum was a natural conclusion to the national office's ongoing objections to bail rejection. Whether SNCC, CORE, or the SCLC were aware of this policy statement is unclear, but presumably it would not have come as a surprise.

Ironically, at the same time that the NAACP was moving to cement a "bail not jail" policy, CORE was planning a campaign against segregated travel facilities that would make the vision of filling southern jails with hundreds of nonviolent protesters a reality. At the height of the Rock Hill jail-in, CORE enthusiastically agreed to launch a campaign to test the 1960 *Boynton v. Virginia* decision prohibiting segregation of terminal facilities for interstate travel. It was dubbed the "Freedom Ride."

Inspiration for the Freedom Ride came from the 1947 Journey of Reconciliation. The Congress of Racial Equality's Gordon Carey saw the *Boynton* decision as an opportunity to launch a similar campaign and spread nonviolent resistance across the South. Unlike the 1947 campaign, which restricted its itinerary to the border South, CORE would venture into the Deep South, including Georgia, Alabama, and Mississippi. Emboldened by the Rock Hill jail-in, CORE resolved to "Fill up the jails, as Gandhi did in India, fill them to bursting if we ha[ve] to."[11]

On May 4, twenty-two Freedom Riders quietly left Washington, D.C. The first ten days of travel were relatively uneventful. As the Riders approached the Deep South, however, violence and harassment became ever more extreme.[12] On May 14, as the Ride approached Birmingham, Alabama, one bus was firebombed just outside of Anniston. On arrival in Birmingham, the second group of Riders were attacked by members of the Ku Klux Klan.[13] Exhausted and war-weary, CORE members resolved to abandon the Freedom Ride and made plans to fly to New Orleans to attend a rally on May 17. It was only with the intervention of the Nashville SNCC group that the campaign continued.

Plans to persist with the Ride were met with determined resistance from both federal and state government. On May 23, after a riot in Montgomery, Alabama, and numerous political u-turns, the Riders finally boarded a bus and, under armed escort, headed for Jackson, Mississippi.[14] One of the twelve Riders later described how "behind all those escorts I felt like the President of the U.S. touring Russia."[15] James Farmer, the director of CORE, and Lucretia Collins were the first to alight from the bus. As they approached the white restrooms, a Jackson policeman stepped forward and arrested them.[16] Despite Robert Kennedy's hopes that the Riders would leave Jackson, a second bus arrived only a short time after the first, and further arrests were made. Farmer, now imprisoned in the county jail, realized that Mississippi had presented them with an opportunity to fill its jails and sent word to CORE's national office that they should keep sending Riders to Jackson.[17]

Much more so than for the Riders who followed, arrest for these first twenty-seven protesters was especially stressful. "I remember one . . . young lady, who just started pulling her hair out. I mean, screaming and stuff like that. Like, 'I'm supposed to be dead,'" recalled Dave Dennis. "We had psyched ourselves to the extent of dying, that this was going to be it. And when it didn't happen . . . we all went through some psychological . . . problems . . . because we had not expected to survive this."[18] The pressure of imprisonment appears to have been particularly intense for the two white men and four black women who were arrested that day: jail segregation meant that they were isolated from the black men, who made up the majority of the group and included all of the older, more experienced activists.[19]

On May 26, the twenty-seven Riders were brought to trial. Judge James Spencer found the accused guilty of breaching the peace and sentenced them to a two-hundred-dollar fine and a sixty-day suspended sentence. At the trial, all twenty-seven abided by their pledge to refuse bail and remain in jail for thirty-nine days, the longest one could stay and still have the right to appeal.[20] The same day that the first protesters were in court, the Freedom Ride Coordinating Committee, consisting of representatives from SCLC, SNCC, and CORE, held its first meeting. The Committee outlined its aim: to place pressure upon Attorney General Robert F. Kennedy in order to ensure that the Interstate Commerce Commission enforced the *Boynton* ruling. They hoped to achieve this by filling the "jails of Montgomery and Jackson in order to keep a sharp image of the issues before the public."[21] The realization that Mississippi would continue to imprison the Freedom Riders marked a new phase in the campaign. It had become, in Farmer's words, "a different and far grander thing than we had intended."[22] His prediction would soon prove true: by the end of the summer, a total of 328 Freedom Riders had been imprisoned in Mississippi.

The day before CORE, SNCC, and SCLC came together to secure the success of the Freedom Rides, the NAACP had issued an official position on the project. Their memorandum pledged firm support for the project, called for federal protection, and rejected any demand for a moratorium on the Rides. Such a cordial message was perhaps partly an attempt to repair the damage done by a report in *Jet* stating that, in a speech in Raleigh, North Carolina, Thurgood Marshall had attacked CORE for not defending in court its members arrested as a result of the Rides. The Congress of Racial Equality had responded to this "low blow" by casting it as yet another example of "how the NAACP attempts to embarrass other groups in the civil rights field." In reality, Marshall's speech had not been so much an attack on CORE as a statement of the NAACP's philosophical and pragmatic objections to the idea that "you can test a law and get it thrown out by staying in jail." Nevertheless, it once again heightened awareness of just how profoundly opposed the NAACP was to the rejection of bail.[23]

The arrival of nine Riders in Jackson on May 28 and a further seventeen the following day forced Governor Ross Barnett to confront the possibility of imprisoning protesters en masse. With the Jackson City Jail already overflowing, twenty-two of the prisoners were moved to the county farm, where they were soon joined by other Riders who continued to arrive in Jackson. The prospect of hundreds of civil rights prisoners left Barnett with the deepest fear that any violence against them would bring hundreds more to Mississippi and lead to federal intervention.[24] Such fear was heightened by news reports that Reverend C. T. Vivian had been beaten with a blackjack by Superintendent Max Thomas for refusing to say "sir" to his captors. Mississippi authorities feigned concern regarding these complaints of brutality by suspending Thomas while the case was investigated. He quietly returned to work days later after it was concluded that he had acted in self-defense.[25]

Meanwhile, an attempt to fill Montgomery's jails had collapsed. At least fifteen Riders were arrested and imprisoned in Montgomery during the first week of the Rides, including Ralph Abernathy, Fred Shuttlesworth, and Wyatt T. Walker. The Montgomery arrests, however, had failed to gain the same level of press attention as those in Jackson, and relatively violence-free Jackson must have seemed a more attractive destination than previously riot-torn Montgomery. On June 2, four black Freedom Riders, part of a group traveling to Jackson, used the white waiting room at the Trailways Station in Montgomery without arrest.[26] From then on, all efforts were concentrated upon Jackson.

As early as June 4, the *Jackson Daily News* reported that the civil rights prisoners might be moved to "Parchman Farm," the notorious state penitentiary.[27] News of the intended transfer, leaked to them by a black trusty—"They're going to try to whip your ass"—sent a wave of fear among the prisoners.[28] On June 14, the Board of Commissioners of the Mississippi State Penitentiary called a special meeting to discuss the situation facing them. The city jail and now the county farm were full of civil rights prisoners, and the most obvious fix was to transfer them to the state penitentiary. (In the minutes of that meeting no reference was made to civil rights activists, only to "convicts of misdemeanors.") The commissioners concluded that the Maximum Security Unit and First-Offenders Camp were surplus to their requirements, and that control of these areas should be relinquished to Hinds County in order that "certain named prisoners" could be transferred to the penitentiary. The Hinds County Circuit Court approved these transfers, finding them justified on the basis that it was unable to provide the facilities needed to "properly house its convicts of misdemeanors." Clearly, prison authorities hoped that the threat of the penitentiary might deter new Riders.[29] Hinds County wasted no time in taking control of its allotted section of Parchman. The following day, the first of many groups of Riders made the 130-mile journey to "little Alcatraz." Fear ran high as the group of men caught their first glimpse of Parchman: "the most fabled state prison in the South." "When we arrived [at Parchman]," recalled Dion T. Diamond, "there was an outer ring of barbed wire, steel-meshed fence; ten feet further within . . . a fence . . . that . . . was electrically charged, inside of that was a brick wall." Upon leaving the paddy wagon, the Riders were forced to undress. They were handed prison uniforms, with the smallest going to the largest of the men and vice versa. They were then placed in cells with cellmates of the same size to prevent them from exchanging their clothes.[30]

This was the first, and only, case of civil rights workers being imprisoned in a state penitentiary. The environment in which they found themselves was far different from that of either a city or county jail. Parchman was home to Mississippi's most serious criminals, including those awaiting execution. Accounts by civil rights workers of their imprisonment abound with stories of converting hostile prisoners to their side, but they could never win over everyone.[31] What made relations with the wider prison population of even greater importance was the participation of white Freedom Riders. While white activists had been imprisoned before this point, the majority of civil rights prisoners had been African American. It was only during the summer of 1961 that the civil rights jail experience became a truly integrated affair. Clearly, for these white protesters, hostility from their cellmates was a far greater risk than for African Americans. One white convict imprisoned during the Rides recalled, "we wanted to kick their asses." (No doubt this was something of an understatement.) One African American who had been imprisoned in Parchman during that summer spoke of how "we [the black convicts] were really pretty ignorant about things back then and weren't especially fond of [the Freedom Riders]."[32] Governor Barnett was desperate to avoid both violence and any conversions of the prisoner population; he ordered that the Riders be isolated in the maximum-security unit, with some placed on death row.[33] Isaac Reynolds, a Rider who spent sixty days on death row, recalled that prison guards would open the door to the execution room in an effort to "break" the prisoners. It is ironic that the Freedom Riders brought integration to Parchman for the first time when black and white prisoners were housed in the same death row cellblock.[34]

Restricted in their ability to conventionally punish the Riders, the guards resorted to more covert tactics. "They knew many of us were chain smokers," James Farmer recalled. "They wouldn't allow any cigarettes in, and the guards would walk down the corridors blowing cigarette smoke into our cells. . . . And they knew that most of these were college students. They wouldn't allow any books in, no books whatever."[35] In particular, the persistent singing of freedom songs by the detainees caused many confrontations with the guards. Another punishment consisted of taking away mattresses, leaving the Riders to sleep on bare metal beds. On one occasion, a number of the men refused to give up their mattresses. Guards dragged them the length of the prison on their mattresses and used wrist breakers before they were finally able to detach them. During the day, the windows were closed and the prisoners left to swelter in the heat, while at night they were soaked with fire hoses and then subjected to cold air from fans. "I didn't know Mississippi could get that cold," one commented. "Almost everybody came down with a cold."[36] It is interesting to note that the female Riders escaped the worst of the treatment, although their living conditions varied little from those of the men. It was not until a large number of women (although they only ever comprised one quarter of the total number jailed) went on a hunger strike, demanding that they receive the same treatment as the men, that some were transferred to Parchman. This disparity appears to have been largely due to fear of bad publicity; the authorities perhaps believed that reports of women being beaten would be even more damaging than news of similar violence against men.[37]

The desire to fill Jackson's jails and prisons meant that the Freedom Ride Coordinating Committee was forced to search for an ever-increasing number of volunteers.[38] The difficulty of such a task should not be underestimated: persuading individuals, who often had little or no experience with civil rights protest, to enter a southern jail for thirty-nine days was no easy thing. With the Committee concentrating upon the volume of volunteers, there were occasions when unsuitable people were accepted as Riders. Despite extensive training in the principles of nonviolence prior to arriving in Jackson, many were unprepared for what lay ahead of them. Some new arrivals soon asked for CORE to bail them out, having discovered life as a civil rights prisoner to be far more difficult than they had imagined. The first arrestees tended to be predominantly (sixty-two percent) African American, male, and southern. Attracting the attention of both the media and the federal government was essential to the success of the Rides, and the Committee recognized that they would have a much greater impact if they could recruit both black and white volunteers from across the United States. By July, the Committee had been largely successful: the month's arrestees included almost equal numbers of black and white men. Furthermore, one quarter of all prisoners were women. Almost half of all Riders at this point came from outside the South, and included a Dutchman, a Belgian, a Canadian, and an Austrian.[39] While the 1964 Freedom Summer would mark the most effective recruitment of "outsiders" into the movement, arrest statistics during the month of July reflect the fact that the Freedom Rides attracted a considerable proportion of supporters from outside the South. At the same time, it is also apparent that the Rides attracted a small but significant number of local African Americans. All twelve of those arrested on July 6 were black men who provided residential addresses in Jackson, and all claimed to have been born in Mississippi. Three days later, eleven arrestees were likewise listed as residing in Jackson. All but one had been born in Mississippi, and eight had been born in Jackson or the surrounding area. These "local people" were young, aged between 15 and 21; however, they do not appear to have been college students. Only one had any college education, with the rest listed as having completed between seventh and eleventh grade. In contrast, a significant proportion of Freedom Riders from outside the South, whether white or black, were listed as having attended college. The precise mechanisms by which these Jackson residents were recruited are unknown, nor is it clear whether they were the only local African Americans imprisoned; nevertheless, the presence, even in small numbers, of members of the local black community reflects a highly diverse body of prisoners.[40]

Early in the project, the Freedom Ride Coordinating Committee learned that local support was a vital ingredient in a successful jail-in. The small gifts of food and blankets that locals brought to the jail helped maintain the morale of the jailed, encouraging them to maintain their commitment to the movement. In Jackson, a group of local African American women named Womenpower Unlimited provided the main body of this support. The group, established by Claire Collins Harvey, evolved into an interracial network of three hundred women who brought supplies to the jail and relayed information to the families of imprisoned Riders.[41] Those in Parchman, 130 miles outside of Jackson, could not benefit from such daily deliveries of food. On his visit to Parchman, Governor Barnett told Farmer, "we want you to stay in there and rot. . . . We got to feed you. . . . But we can make that food so damn unpalatable that you can't eat it." Salt, glass, and cleaning powder were all added to the Riders' food.[42] The stresses of prison life, particularly for those least prepared, took their toll upon the Freedom Riders. The division between those philosophically committed to nonviolence and those who merely saw it as a tactic was as evident in the jails and prisons as anywhere else. Arguments broke out regularly over any number of issues: religious worship, hunger strikes, philosophy, even the level of noise in the cell. On a number of occasions, fistfights broke out when one person aggravated those who were fasting by noisily slurping food. Although Farmer organized a democratic system of voting to resolve these differences, on the whole people appear to have behaved however they felt appropriate. Some refused to cooperate with prison authorities in any way. Others simply sought to get through the experience with their mental and physical health intact.[43] While state and county authorities largely prevented violence against the Riders to avoid federal intervention, the dangers of imprisonment remained very real. Authorities certainly did not prevent all violence from occurring, and no doubt welcomed the culture of intimidation and fear that evolved. The *threat* of violence—the knowledge of what *might* happen—was enough to place some Riders under immense psychological pressure.

Although some Riders found aspects of jail life difficult, the majority did stay for the full thirty-nine days, and some stayed longer. For many the experience was transformative. Around half of the jailed Riders were African American, and three quarters of these were men. As African American men were most commonly the victims of unjust convictions, many found imprisonment to be a liberating experience. Having survived prison, they felt that they could survive anything. On the other hand, the experience gave Northern white students an opportunity to feel firsthand what African Americans had to endure every day. Thirty-nine days of imprisonment "is nothing compared to the lifetime of suffering and embarrassment that twenty million Americans must face because their skin is black," wrote one white student to Farmer.[44] One of the few "luxuries" allowed the Riders was the freedom to write home to their parents and friends. For Riders from the North, these often highly emotional letters communicated the plight of southern African Americans in a very personal manner. On occasion, they also inspired parents to publicize events in the South by circulating copies of the letters and holding fund-raising events.[45] Regardless of race or gender, imprisonment created a shared experience and common purpose among the Freedom Riders. "The feeling of people coming out of the jail was one that they had triumphed, that they had achieved," C. T. Vivian noted. "Nonviolence was proven in that respect."[46] The leveling nature of jail was an important asset to the movement, and it enabled both blacks and whites to make a genuine sacrifice.

In July it was reported that the Hinds County representative, Russell Davis, would ask the state legislature to cover the cost of jailing the Riders. Allen Thompson, mayor of Jackson, estimated that the protests had cost the city of Jackson two hundred and fifty thousand dollars. Plans to abolish an "auto-use tax" in Jackson that summer had to be abandoned. Jailing and prosecuting the 328 Riders was clearly a costly operation for Hinds County. Just how much financial pressure the Riders placed on the county is difficult to estimate: while the aforementioned figure could have been inflated to encourage further hostility toward the Riders, Mayor Thompson actually opposed Davis's actions and stated that Hinds County did not want any such help. The inference is that the county resented the implication that it could not deal with challenges to segregation by itself.[47] It seems unlikely that the Riders ever really came close to forcing the Jackson authorities to stop arresting those who challenged segregation merely through financial pressure. During the early weeks of the Freedom Rides, the media swarmed into Jackson, waiting to see how white Mississippi would respond to this unprecedented challenge to its way of life. Allowing the Riders the symbolic victory of integrating the bus station facilities was a cost that the authorities were not prepared to bear. Simultaneously, with the media watching, official violence could precipitate federal intervention—an equally costly option. Under these circumstances, the authorities clearly decided that mass imprisonment of the Riders was the only option open to them.[48]

The question of who would assume the financial burden of imprisoning the Riders remained open through 1961. It arose as a major concern for the state penitentiary's Board of Commissioners when they met on November 14. While Hinds County had agreed to bear the cost of imprisoning the Riders, by the time of the meeting, the penitentiary still had not been reimbursed. The financial status of the penitentiary was of grave concern to the commissioners that November. The prison was running at a deficit, and it was suggested that programs would have to be cut unless further income was appropriated from the Mississippi legislature. (Precisely what these "programs" were was not stated.) Indeed, it would appear that the state penitentiary had already been facing financial difficulties before the summer of 1961. It was believed to be overstaffed, and plans had been drawn up to make fifteen members of staff redundant. The arrival of the Riders, however, forced these plans to be delayed.[49]

Few Freedom Riders were incarcerated for longer than thirty-nine days—a fact that must have helped ease the financial burden of imprisoning them. By July, 196 Riders had been released on bail, pending appeal. Thus far, the bail bill stood at $138,000. On August 4, Mississippi authorities ordered all 196 Riders to return to Jackson within ten days for their appeals to be heard. All but six did so, at which point the authorities announced that they would be tried two at a time. The majority returned home, again at CORE's expense. No doubt in the hope of bankrupting CORE, the Mississippi court responded to the appeals by doubling the prison sentence to four months and tripling the fine to $1,500. The Congress of Racial Equality was left close to financial ruin. The situation was only resolved when the $372,000 in fines and bail was cleared by a loan from the NAACP Legal Defense Fund.[50]

The Congress of Racial Equality's decision to appeal the convictions in court was not only financially costly, but it also brought profound implications for the organization's commitment to nonviolence. In spite of the Miami and Rock Hill jail-ins, and months of discussion on the need to commit to long prison terms, it had adopted what was effectively a tactical approach to imprisonment. A great amount of pressure was placed on CORE by the conditions under which protesters were held, and presumably fewer people would have traveled to Jackson if faced with the prospect of imprisonment for months. In effect, CORE's response was a hybrid of legal and nonviolent action. What the Freedom Ride Coordinating Committee called "jail-no-bail" was actually much closer to the NAACP's strategy of challenging segregation in court than most would admit. Marshall had indeed been correct when he said that one cannot "get [a law] thrown out by staying in jail": most Riders accepted bail after thirty-nine days in order to challenge their conviction in court. The Freedom Rides taught the lesson that, in order to attain its true potential, jail-no-bail would have to move away from its strict pacifist ideals and become a more sophisticated, flexible response to segregationist resistance. Nevertheless, one should not understate the importance of the Rides. Not only did they prompt federal intervention, but they also marked the first jailing of an interracial group en masse, and succeeded in effecting change by targeting the criminal justice system of a single city.[51] Furthermore, as John Lewis would later recall, the Freedom Rides transformed and radicalized the movement. They brought hundreds of new supporters from across the country into the South and threw them straight into the belly of the beast: Parchman Farm.[52] Having survived Parchman, many were ready to keep on fighting. The Freedom Riders forever changed the relationship between the civil rights movement and imprisonment—they took the movement inside the prison and ensured that imprisonment was no longer a byproduct of racial protest, but a tactic in itself. Furthermore, there were long-term consequences of the Freedom Rides for Mississippi's prison system. Shortly after the protesters' release, lawyers from the Legal Defense Fund brought damage actions over their clients' treatment in Parchman. They subsequently broadened their assault upon conditions in the penitentiary in *Gates v. Collier*, which challenged the treatment and segregation of all prisoners.[53] This was an important example of how the imprisonment of civil rights activists drew the movement into a broader challenge to the southern penal system. In the years to come, such efforts would be greatly expanded, and they produced some important institutional reforms.

In February 1962, with the Freedom Riders still released on bail, CORE came together to discuss how they should respond to imprisonment in the future. Those present agreed that jail-no-bail campaigns should be organized according to whether they were "long-term," such as the Freedom Rides, or "community jail-ins," as in the case of the Rock Hill campaign. Reflecting upon the experiences of jailed Freedom Riders, the committee decided that future long-term jail-ins should have a predetermined leader, responsible for maintaining discipline, assigned to each of the four groups of prisoners (black and white, men and women). These leaders would also play an important role in educating participants in the realities of jail life, particularly the attendant psychological pressures. Drawing upon the lessons of the Rock Hill campaign, the committee stressed the need for extensive planning before initiating any further community jail-ins. In particular, they called upon organizers to establish a community-wide level of support before courting imprisonment.[54] The Congress of Racial Equality's discussion of jail-no-bail reflected a much more sophisticated understanding of the mechanics of jail-ins than that possessed by either SNCC or SCLC. Yet, for all of its experience, and despite the success of the Freedom Rides, CORE sought to maintain its pacifist credentials and remained troubled by the Riders' acceptance of bail. Indeed, a suggestion was even made that the bonded Riders should return to Mississippi to court arrest again in order to serve a full prison sentence.[55]

The Freedom Rides marked the height of the jail-in movement. The campaign not only brought an important victory for CORE, but it also cemented the jail experience as a crucial part of civil rights movement identity. In the years to come, the term "Freedom Rider" was used to describe the most determined and defiant civil rights activists, regardless of whether they had actually been a part of the campaign. Yet, if the Freedom Rides marked a vindication of the jail-in strategy, it was never repeated on the same scale. Although attempts to fill the jails would continue for many years, the belief that one could transform the South via imprisonment lost influence after 1961. At the forefront of these changes were SNCC and CORE, both of whom turned toward community organizing and voter registration as the main focus of their work in the months after the Freedom Riders were released. The increasing emphasis upon community organizing made it much more difficult to utilize mass imprisonment as a protest strategy. But this was certainly not the end of the jail experience. Indeed, more arrests took place between 1962 and 1964 than had in the preceding two years. However, most local activists simply could not afford to remain in jail for any period of time. Furthermore, while many willingly entered jail as part of their fight against white supremacy, they could not always share the Freedom Riders' view of imprisonment as a liberating, positive experience. As white repression and violence escalated, the movement struggled to maintain these philosophical and ideological aspects of jail-no-bail. Increasingly, activists were forced to weigh the strategic benefits of accepting jail versus the immense personal danger that imprisonment brought. The following chapter explores these developments within three southern communities at a time when going to jail became a truly mass experience for activists. Ironically, while this was an achievement that SNCC, CORE, and SCLC had all once aspired toward, it also greatly undermined the earlier vision of filling the jails as a prime aspiration of the nonviolent movement. In the years to come, CORE's acceptance that they needed to recognize the varied needs of incarcerated activists and develop a flexible response to legal repression was well and truly tested.

4

The Middle of the Iceberg

"We are smuggling this note from the drunk tank of the county jail in Magnolia, Mississippi. Twelve of us are here, sprawled out along the concrete bunker . . . I'm sitting here with smuggled pen and paper, thinking a little, writing a little," wrote SNCC's Bob Moses in November 1961. "Later on Hollis will lead out with a clear tenor into a freedom song, Talbert and Lewis will supply jokes, and McDew will discourse on the history of the black man and the Jew. . . . This is Mississippi, the middle of the iceberg. . . . This is a tremor in the middle of the iceberg—from a stone that the builders rejected."[1] On October 31, Moses, along with other SNCC workers and local students from Mc-Comb, had been found guilty of disturbing the peace and contributing to the delinquency of minors. They had received sentences lasting from four to six months. Moses wrote his letter while in the county jail, and shortly after had it smuggled out to the SNCC office. The group remained incarcerated for five weeks while those on the outside tried to raise the fourteen-thousand-dollar bail.

Moses had first arrived in McComb in mid-July to assist local activist C. C. Bryant with voter registration. August was spent working alongside John Hardy and Reginald Robinson. They walked from house to house, talking to local black residents about voter registration, and trying to convince them that they were committed to remaining in McComb despite a series of violent attacks against civil rights workers that month. The focus on voter registration had recently been given further impetus when the Kennedy administration offered SNCC private funding to aid such work. Some SNCC members objected to the proposal, believing that the offer was an attempt to channel organizing efforts away from the open confrontations associated with direct-action protest. Others argued that increasing the political power of black communities was pivotal to the fight against white supremacy. Black disfranchisement affected almost every aspect of life: from the standard of education to the exclusion of African Americans from juries. The dispute was eventually resolved with the formation of two separate wings within the group, one specializing in direct action and the other in voter registration.[2] At the end of August more SNCC workers arrived, including Marion Barry and Charles Sherrod from the newly formed direct-action wing. They set about organizing nonviolent protests with local high school students Hollis Watkins and Curtis Hayes. The protests, however, soon ground to a halt when Hayes and Watkins were arrested. The following day, a further three students were arrested during a protest at the Greyhound bus terminal. On September 5, the campaign received an even greater blow when a member of the Mississippi state legislature, E. H. Hurst, shot and killed Herbert Lee. Lee had been a member of the NAACP, and had helped Moses contact potential voter registrants. Hurst claimed that Lee had attacked him, but the SNCC workers knew that Lee had been murdered as a result of his civil rights work. The following week, the five students arrested in nonviolent protests were released after spending thirty-four days in the county jail. When the principal of the local high school refused to admit two of them, the students marched out of school and to the SNCC office, where they announced their determination to march through town. As they prayed at the steps of city hall, police began making arrests. A hostile crowd had gathered, and they began to viciously beat Bob Zellner, the only white protester, as local police and Federal Bureau of Investigation agents looked on. A total of 116 students were arrested. Ninety-seven of the prisoners, who were under eighteen years of age, were released. The remaining nineteen, along with nine SNCC workers, ended up in Magnolia County Jail, where Moses wrote his much-cited letter.

Starting with Moses's work in McComb in 1961, civil rights workers spread throughout southern communities to help organize nonviolent protests and voter registration. For SNCC and CORE, in particular, large-scale campaigns such as the Freedom Rides no longer held as much appeal. The focus was now on grassroots organizing and developing local leadership. From late 1961, as the nonviolent movement spread throughout communities, serving jail time became a truly mass experience. This chapter surveys three of those communities: Albany, Georgia; Jackson, Mississippi; and Americus, Georgia. The movements in these places highlight the continuing influence of gender on the jail experience, the treatment of prisoners, and conflict over how to respond to arrest and imprisonment. They also demonstrate the tremendous financial, moral, and physical pressure that was put upon individuals, organizations, and the civil rights movement in general by the increasingly serious charges made against activists.

In the fall of 1961, Charles Sherrod and Cordell Reagon arrived by bus in Albany, Georgia. They had the lessons from McComb fresh in their minds, and plans to establish a voter registration project. They also faced an uphill struggle to overcome the climate of fear they encountered within the black community. Although Albany, compared to surrounding rural counties, had a relatively peaceful history of race relations, its black residents nevertheless lived under rigid segregation. Albany's criminal justice system served a crucial role in maintaining this inequality. A 1962 report on Albany described how "The entire machinery of justice in the city and county is capable of instantaneous conversion into a machinery for repression where Negroes are involved—for the judge, juries, prosecuting attorneys, sheriffs, deputies, city police, are all white."[3] The Albany campaign itself arose in the shadow of attempts by local African American lawyer Chevene King to indict Sheriff Johnson of "Bad" Baker County for violating the civil rights of local plantation worker Charlie Ware. Ware had been arrested upon the orders of his white plantation overseer after he flirted with the overseer's African American mistress. Shouting down his radio transmitter that the handcuffed Ware had attacked him, Johnson shot the field hand three times in the neck. Ware staged a miraculous recovery, whereupon he was indicted for felonious assault.[4]

Sherrod, Reagon, and the newly arrived Charles Jones soon focused their attention upon the youth of the city, much to the disdain of the local NAACP leadership, which greeted the arrival of the SNCC workers with both suspicion and hostility.[5] On November 1, the day the Interstate Commerce Commission's order against the segregation of terminal facilities came into effect, nine volunteers used the white waiting room in the Albany bus station. It was an inauspicious start to a campaign that would see the arrest of thousands of Albany residents. Nevertheless, it secured the attention of both Albany's whites and the local black leadership. Fearful that SNCC would now eclipse their control of the community, the NAACP, community leaders, and SNCC representatives came together under the auspices of the Albany Movement. Community leaders William Anderson and Slater King were elected as president and vice president. To date there had been no arrests. The NAACP, no doubt deeply conscious of the fate of Charlie Ware, hoped it would be able to suppress demonstrations and keep the Albany citizenry out of jail.[6] Such hopes, however, were dashed only days later when three high school students were arrested for refusing to leave the white section of the Albany bus station. Shortly afterward, two students at Albany State College followed suit and were also arrested. While the two high school students were bailed out within the hour, the Albany State students remained in jail through Thanksgiving night.

It was the arrest of nine Freedom Riders on Sunday, December 10 that finally brought mass arrests. The group of Riders had traveled to Albany from Atlanta to test the facilities at the local bus station. Police chief Laurie Pritchett immediately arrested eight of the Freedom Riders, along with Charles Jones and two local students, Bertha Gober and Wilma Henderson. They were charged with "creating an obstruction," and all refused to be released on bail. Within weeks, Martin Luther King had joined hundreds of Albany residents in jail and focused national attention upon the city. "We shall overcome!" shouted Charles Sherrod as he marched to jail. This was *it*, Sherrod believed: they would finally get the chance to fill the jails.[7] Convincing members of the adult population to share such a view of imprisonment, however, was difficult. Local people had been imprisoned in campaigns before Albany, but this had not been en masse, nor had they represented a cross-section of the black community.

While the arrest of the Freedom Riders clearly rallied support for the Albany Movement, it was the arrest the following day of the much-respected Marion King as she prayed outside city hall that shocked the black community into action.[8] Two days later, a mass march attracted a far greater number of adults, including many from the working classes. So far, Pritchett had only arrested protest leaders—the arrest of 267 marchers that day therefore came as a shock. After further arrests the following day, 471 people were imprisoned.[9] Pritchett, however, was not prepared to allow the movement to fill the jails. Days earlier, he had contacted jailers in the surrounding counties, making arrangements for them to house civil rights prisoners.[10] That evening, hundreds of those arrested were placed in vans and dispersed throughout the surrounding counties. The news that they were being taken out of Albany to areas notorious for their brutal police and violent treatment of locals terrified the prisoners. "You're not in Albany any more. You're in Camilla," one group of prisoners was told.[11] In Camilla Jail, sixteen-year-old Annie Sue Herring was slapped by a guard for refusing to call him "sir," then told, "that's just a sample of what you're going to get." She reported that most of the men and boys with her received similar treatment.[12] In Dawson Jail, Sheriff Matthews punched a SNCC worker when he asked for time to be set aside for prayer.[13] Later, Slater King had his head rammed into iron bars for giving his breakfast to a fellow prisoner.[14]

As Albany's black community exploded in protest, the Freedom Riders, having been tried on charges of disorderly conduct, obstructing the flow of traffic, and failure to obey an officer on December 12, were found guilty and returned to jail. Joan Browning was the only white woman within the group, and was therefore alone. For white women in the civil rights movement, jail segregation meant that their incarceration could often be a lonely time. Crucial to maintaining morale was the ability to communicate with her friends. One of the jail trusties, Willie, delivered notes written on scraps of paper towel with messages such as "we are winning," "keep the faith," and "we shall overcome." In letters to a friend, however, the pressures of jail—compounded by being on hunger strike—are evident. On Monday, December 18 she wrote: "I'm becoming depressed myself now but I can't let anyone know it. This morning two guys came in, one big and red-faced with a cigar to suggest that I eat. I finally got a glass of water, my first since Thursday. It is now 96+ hours since I ate." Occasionally, the isolation of the white women's cell was punctuated by the arrival of a new inmate, most often drunk. Asked by one if she was "one of those 'damned freedom riders,'" Browning feared that she was about to suffer her first beating.[15] The experience of being incarcerated evoked mixed emotions for her.[16] "I never dreamed I would be in jail," she recalled. "I was embarrassed to be there, but also proud because I had acted on my beliefs."[17] According to social mores, white women were only incarcerated for the most heinous of crimes. Her decision to flout the rules of southern segregation and associate with the movement certainly violated that code of behavior. Writing to a friend in Atlanta, she observed the impact of her presence in Albany upon local white men: "Rumor has it that I am a special mark. The white men feel that they should take steps to save me from myself and these people I'm with."[18] The idea that Browning had been manipulated into joining the movement was certainly an attractive explanation for her activism.

It preserved the values of southern womanhood while also conforming to gender stereotypes—namely that Browning, as a woman, was unable to act independently. This suggests that Browning's status as a white woman may have offered a degree of protection from segregationist violence; nevertheless, two cases of sexual harassment and abuse of white female civil rights workers in Albany—discussed in greater detail in the next chapter—reflect the fact that this demographic remained vulnerable.[19]

Meanwhile, the jail cells reserved for black women were overflowing. Jane Rambeau was one of those arrested during the first wave of protests. In an interview, she recalled:

> They started to herd us into the jail as fast as they could which was really slow. . . . All the . . . stories [of jail] I heard my parents talk about . . . [were] back . . . like instant replay. At this moment, I [saw] them dragging a young black girl . . . down that gravel walkway and up those steps. . . . And I remember the blood running down her face. I said . . . this got to change. This got to change.

Rambeau was one of the protesters who remained in the Albany jail. "About the second day people started to get really sick."[20] Geneva Collier, a thirty-four-year-old mother, was transported out of Albany. For two weeks she was held in a house in surrounding Lee County with a number of other women. They were kept in "a regular old house . . . it was two to a bed, I had a big old red bed." When Pritchett reportedly had the use of jail facilities within a forty-mile radius of Albany, the fact that some prisoners were held in a house, with all the extra costs of guarding them there, is strange. Collier presumed, "they didn't want to put us [women] in a regular jail." Yet, given the incidences of brutality against black women within the Albany Movement, the most extreme example being the beating of Slater King's pregnant wife, this seems highly unlikely.[21] One must question whether Collier's rather unusual experience was the result of more restrictions on Pritchett's access to the surrounding jails than has previously been reported. The testimony of two local women, Jane Rambeau and Mary

Jones, imprisoned around the same time as Collier, further reinforces this interpretation. Rambeau recalled, "I marched again, again, again. But it had reached a point where they would arrest some people and some people they wouldn't arrest. Well the truth is they didn't have space. . . . There were folks that wanted to go to jail . . . it became expensive trying to get these other counties to take . . . prisoners." Mary Jones recalled that after her first arrest, she did not return to jail "because by the time I got out . . . [there were] so many folks in jail . . . they wasn't locking up no more."[22] At what point during the course of the campaign this occurred is unclear. However, such testimony certainly contradicts the universally accepted belief among historians that the Albany Movement completely failed to fill the jails.[23]

Bernice Johnson Reagon was a student at Albany State College when she became involved in the protests. In an interview she observed that "Albany settled the issue of whether to go to jail. Songs helped to do that, because in the songs you could just name the people who were trying to use this against you—Asa Kelley, who was the mayor, Chief Pritchett, who was the police."[24] Reagon was not alone in observing the strong association between jail and the music of the movement, particularly what became known as freedom songs.[25] While freedom songs were sung in a variety of situations and for a number of reasons, the jail experience nevertheless repeatedly figures as a powerful influence.

With titles such as "We Shall Overcome" and "This Little Light of Mine," freedom songs followed the African American tradition of using song as a form of protest. Albany is often credited with bringing freedom songs to the forefront of the movement, but such songs were certainly an important part of the jail experience before this point. John Lewis recalled singing freedom songs while imprisoned for participating in the Nashville sit-ins in 1960. During the Rock Hill jail-in and the Freedom Rides, incarcerated activists were punished by guards when they refused to stop singing. Accounts of imprisonment by civil rights activists regularly refer to singing as one of the key ways in which they sought to maintain morale and unity. Reagon recalled that during the first wave of arrests in Albany, "the jails were packed with Blacks from all levels of society. . . . One medium of unity and communication with such a group was the songs."[26] Freedom songs not only provided solace to those in jail, they also served a crucial role in communicating a new perspective of imprisonment within the movement.[27] In mass meetings and on marches, members of Albany's black community sang about jail. The spirit of collective action expressed by the lyrics helped overcome the fear of being lost within a brutal system that had long been used to isolate those who challenged the white power structure.

"I Ain't Scared of Your Jail" addressed the question of imprisonment more directly than any other song. In *Everybody Says Freedom*, Pete Seeger and Bob Reiser describe a mass march in Birmingham, Alabama, at which those about to be arrested used the song to declare that jail would not end their struggle. Speaking at a mass meeting before the protest, Fred Shuttlesworth warned: "It's to be a silent demonstration. . . . No songs, no slogans, no replies to obscenities. . . . However," he continued, "when you're arrested, sing your hearts out." The marchers silently filed out of the church, remaining quiet until police approached the group and ordered their arrest. The hundreds of marchers then burst into song:

Ain't a-scared of your jail 'cause I want my freedom.[28]

The simple act of declaring that jail was no longer a feared place was liberating. This statement of liberation was taken further, however, by also claiming that only imprisonment could bring African Americans the freedom they craved. Such a seemingly contradictory association lay at the heart of the movement's attempt to reveal the way in which entire communities were imprisoned by a brutal system of white supremacy that robbed African Americans of their self-respect and held them captive to their own fear. By openly discussing the fear people felt toward jail within freedom songs, the movement sought to give new meaning to imprisonment: jail would become a physical and symbolic battleground.

As Christmas approached in Albany, local jails were alive with the sound of freedom songs. Over five hundred people had already been arrested, and others were replacing them. The SCLC's Bernard Lee marveled at their resilience. Maids gave false names to conceal news of their arrest from employers; children were arrested, only to be released and to rejoin the protests.[29] In an article written for the *New University of Chicago News*, James Forman wrote passionately of his pride in Albany's black residents: "People were exposing themselves to the dirt of their city—its jails. They were placed twenty to thirty in a cell made for four. They saw amongst their numbers, pregnant women, sick men and hungry children suffering for what they considered Freedom."[30] It gradually became clear, however, that the movement was facing a problem: no matter how committed people were to going to jail initially, many soon requested bail. By December 15, two hundred people had been bailed out, and the Albany Movement had exhausted its funds. With media attention on Albany and local protesters unsure as to how to cope with the situation, William Anderson, president of the Albany Movement, contacted the SCLC office in Atlanta to request assistance. While it remains unclear exactly how much support existed for such a move, at some point Martin Luther King agreed that he would travel to Albany.[31]

Although there was a vibrant and growing campaign in Albany prior to King's arrival, it nevertheless marked a new phase for both the SCLC and the local movement. Despite opposition to King moving into Albany, he potentially offered the benefits of both cash and media attention.[32] Furthermore, in a situation where many were desperate to leave jail, news of King's imminent arrival provided a crucial psychological boost. "Word came to us in jail that Martin Luther King was coming to Albany and I can never forget the excitement," recalled Jane Rambeau. "That sort of gave us courage to go and stay [in jail] a few more days because we had some body that was going to see . . . us."[33] The arrival of King on December 16, as well as his subsequent arrest during a mass march the next day, had a powerful impact upon the local community and media coverage of the movement, but it did not resolve the many challenges the Albany Movement was facing. With more than seven hundred people in jail and Christmas approaching, Marion Page, Charles Sherrod, and Chevene and Slater

King were weary and somewhat resentful of the way in which Martin Luther King's imprisonment had placed him in the limelight. On December 18, an agreement was made that the protesters would be freed and, in exchange for a thirty-day moratorium on demonstrations, a vague promise was given that negotiations would take place at some point in the future. According to David Lewis, the truce was signed in a confused effort to reestablish the original power dynamics of the movement by forcing King's departure.[34] It is clear, however, that, at a meeting of the movement's executive committee to discuss the proposed agreement, news of jail conditions weighed very heavily on people's minds. The NAACP's Ruby Hurley brought news that one traumatized girl had been under sedation ever since her release from a rat-infested cell. Charles Jones argued that further demonstrations could bring the rapid desegregation of the city, but most do not appear to have shared his optimism and were instead swayed by Hurley's insistence that the protesters be released.[35] Upon his release from jail, King described the settlement as a "hoax"; nevertheless, he was evidently keen to be released. In *Parting the Waters*, Taylor Branch recounts that William Anderson, in jail with King, was suffering a nervous breakdown. Anderson's ramblings, including proclamations to King that "You are Jesus," convinced the SCLC leader that Anderson could not withstand the pressure of jail any longer, and King seized upon the settlement as a way to leave jail.[36]

News of Anderson's condition was not shared with those outside the SCLC's upper echelons. King's failure to stay in jail fuelled SNCC members' resentment of his messianic leadership style. "De Lawd," as SNCC members had christened King, had still not spent a prolonged period in jail. Diane Nash, one of the foremost members of the Nashville contingent and well-known for her unflinching commitment to Gandhian nonviolence, was particularly disappointed by King's acceptance of bail. In February 1960, when Nash was arrested in Nashville during sit-in protests, she caused an uproar when she informed the judge that she and fifteen others would go to jail rather than pay a fine. This was the first case of students rejecting bail, and it played an important role in popularizing the concept of jail-no-bail. By April 1962, however, Nash—now five months pregnant with her first child—felt that the nonviolent movement as a whole had abandoned its commitment to filling the jails. Frustrated by activists' cooperation with legal authorities, she decided to drop her appeal against a two-year prison sentence for contributing to the delinquency of minors while working in McComb, Mississippi. She announced in a statement to the press:

> I believe the time has come when each of us must make up his mind, when arrested on unjust charges, to serve his sentence and stop posting bonds. . . . We in the non-violent movement have been talking about jail without bail for two years or more. It is time for us to do what we say . . . I think we all realize what it would mean if we had hundreds and thousands of people across the South prepared to go to jail and stay. There can be no doubt that our battle would be won. . . . We have faltered and hesitated.

Nash would not only give birth in a Mississippi jail, but also stood to miss the first year of her child's life. In a statement to the press, Nash placed her decision to go to jail within the context of her duty as a mother: "Since my child will be a black child, born in Mississippi, whether I am in jail or not he will be born in prison. I believe that if I go to jail now it may help hasten that day when my child and all children will be free."[37] By referring directly to her duty as a mother in order to justify her decision, Nash created a powerful image of black children being trapped inside a white-controlled world from the moment they were born. By allowing them to imprison both herself and her unborn baby, she directly challenged Mississippi authorities in order to expose the true hypocrisy and injustice of the system.

News of Nash's imminent imprisonment spread throughout the movement and Mississippi: here was a young, well-educated, pregnant woman requesting a two-year jail sentence. Judge Moore, presiding over Nash's case, was horrified at the attention that her imprisonment would bring to the Magnolia State. He turned first to Nash's new husband, James Bevel, in hopes he could persuade him to intervene. Bevel responded characteristically to this appeal by explaining: "Judge Moore, you don't understand Christianity. . . . All the early Christians went to jail." "Maybe so," Moore responded, "But they weren't all pregnant and twenty-one." When his efforts came to naught, Moore simply declined to impose the two-year sentence. Nash ended up serving only ten days in jail for refusing to move to the side of the courtroom reserved for blacks.[38]

Nash was far from the only mother who voluntarily marched into jail. Women formed the backbone of the movement in communities throughout the South. They housed workers, canvassed homes, marched through the streets, and were arrested.[39] Many local female activists were mothers, and for them going to jail usually meant leaving their children behind. Geneva Collier recalled being imprisoned for two weeks in Albany, forcing her husband to care for their six children: "my husband was trying to get me out 'cause he had to see about the children."[40] Set within a historical context, this was a significant reversal of gender roles. For decades, the common pattern had been that men—husbands, fathers—were imprisoned, meaning women had to raise their children alone.

The movement in Albany continued to push for change throughout 1962, but with little success. In July, King and Abernathy returned to face the charges brought against them the preceding December. On July 10, Judge Durden found King and Abernathy guilty of parading without a permit. King, aware that his response to the verdict could make or break both the Albany campaign and his leadership of the civil rights movement, announced that he would not pay the $178 fine. He would stay in jail for the full forty-five-day sentence.[41] In his autobiography, Ralph Abernathy recalled the filthy conditions of their cell in Albany Jail: "The cell we stepped into was the filthiest place I had ever seen. Martin and I looked at one another in disbelief. . . . The floor was concrete, as best we could tell, but it was covered by a coat of scum and dirt. . . . [The toilet] was also caked with scum, and the bottom was encrusted with rust. . . . We later learned that we were enjoying special privileges because we were celebrities. The rest of the demonstrators were crammed eight and ten in a cell." Just as local women had provided the Freedom Riders in Jackson with food, so the people of Albany rallied around the imprisoned protesters. "From that moment on we were never without food in the cell," recalled Abernathy. "Not only did the women bring hot dishes that evening, but they also baked pies, cakes and cookies." Abernathy's recollections of his jail time create the impression that neither he nor King shared the same kind of suffering that the "noncelebrities" of the movement endured.[42]

King's attempt to prove his commitment to jail-going, however, was soon frustrated by Chief Pritchett, who decided to evict King and Abernathy from jail by privately ensuring their fines were paid. It was a serious blow to their efforts to victoriously conclude the campaign.[43] Angered by yet another early exit from jail, and realizing that the SCLC could not withdraw from Albany without some kind of victory, King again resolved to lead a campaign in the town. Negotiations with Pritchett (resumed shortly after King was ejected from jail) soon ran aground and the SCLC, realizing that the police chief had no intention of providing concessions, planned a mass rally for the night of July 18. A few hours before the crowds assembled, however, Judge Elliott, a Kennedy-appointed federal judge, issued an injunction against demonstrations.[44] For King, the question of whether to defy a federal order was deeply problematic. At the heart of the problem for the SCLC was the fact that, to date, they had never committed an act of civil disobedience against the *federal* government.[45] Defiance of the federal injunction would not only run the risk of imprisonment for a genuinely illegal act, but it would also undermine the movement's concept of imprisonment as moral protest and a badge of honor. In the end, the question was sidestepped. The injunction had only been issued against King, Abernathy, and Anderson; hence, on the night of July 18, a local leader headed the mass march. Only a few days later, Judge Tuttle dissolved the injunction on the grounds that it was unconstitutional. King's third arrest on July 24 failed to push negotiations forward. Hundreds of protesters were still in jail, and at a meeting of five hundred activists that night, only fifteen volunteered to join Charles Sherrod and submit to imprisonment. The black community's readiness to spend time in jail had evidently disappeared, and without that there could be no more mass marches.[46] By mid-August, most of the outside organizers had left Albany, but local activists continued to battle against the intransigent white power structure for years to come.

Both the SCLC and SNCC had believed that they could apply the example of the Freedom Rides to the situation in Albany. They believed that if they could fill the jails, they would be able to secure concessions from the city. However, as Adam Fairclough observes, they learned that only five percent of a black community could be expected to volunteer to go to jail.[47] Regardless of how the experience empowered individuals, the financial impact of a long stay in jail was simply too great. As Pat Watters commented, "though many [black southerners] were literally starving, most were not down to that sheer edge of desperation [where] they had nothing to lose in the sacrifice."[48] In his own judgment of the campaign, King argued that he had been guilty of focusing too closely on filling the jails. "To rigidly proclaim," he argued, "that the only task [of nonviolent protest] is to fill the jails may well lead the movement under certain conditions into a trap."[49] Others made similar observations. Bill Hansen recalled: "We were naive enough to think that we could fill up the jails. . . . We ran out of people before [Chief Pritchett] ran out of jails."[50] While the campaign cast a long shadow over the future effectiveness of the jail-in, it ensured that the jail experience was no longer the domain of students and the young. The fact that the SCLC felt disappointment that only five percent of black residents could be expected to volunteer for jail should not overshadow just how much this represented a transformation of residents' attitudes.

By December 1962, the city of Jackson, Mississippi, had experienced little civil rights activity since the Freedom Riders were released from jail in the summer of 1961. The Mississippi NAACP, with Medgar Evers at its head, was the only civil rights organization active in the area. That winter, the NAACP Youth Council, helped by a couple of SNCC workers who had remained behind after the Freedom Rides, launched a boycott of downtown stores and made plans to picket Woolworth's. The boycott continued to grow during the early months of 1963, but the NAACP National Office, while expressing its support, would not provide assistance with bail bonds.[51] It was not until May

28, with bail secured from elsewhere, that the movement in Jackson finally entered its direct-action phase. Tougaloo College students and faculty sat in at the Woolworth's lunch counter, whereupon they were attacked by onlookers for two hours before the manager closed the store. Three days later, four hundred high school children walked out of school and held the first mass march of the campaign. Police responded to the protest by arresting all of them.[52] The arrests sparked the first mass response from the local community, and the movement began to gain momentum. Over the next week, hundreds of adults and children were arrested and dispersed across the state to local and county jails, as well as to Parchman Farm. Although only for a brief time, the protesters succeeded in filling Jackson's jails.

The mayor of Jackson responded to the protests and arrests by converting the livestock buildings at the state fairgrounds into prison camps, using garbage trucks to carry the students to their makeshift cells. Anne Moody was one of those sent to the improvised jailhouse.

> We discovered we were headed for the fairgrounds. When we got there, the driver rolled up the windows, turned the heater on, got out, closed the door and left us. . . . Sweat began dripping off us. An hour went by. . . . The compounds they put us in were two large buildings used to auction off cattle during the annual state fair. . . . The openings had been closed up with wire. It reminded me of a concentration camp.[53]

Within days of the Woolworth's sit-in, members of the NAACP National Office started arriving in Jackson. On June 1, Roy Wilkins, Medgar Evers, and NAACP field secretary Helen Wilcher were arrested as they picketed the Woolworth's store.[54] "We've baptized brother Wilkins!" Martin Luther King reportedly exclaimed when he heard the news, perhaps with a touch of irony. Over the following days, a number of telegrams and letters arrived at the NAACP National Office in New York offering their sincere congratulations to the executive secretary for his bold and decisive course of action. One letter exuberantly congratulated Roy Wilkins for joining the ranks of jail-goers: "I couldn't have been more proud of you than I was when the news of your arrest in Jackson, Mississippi flashed across the television screen on Saturday night."[55] Hopes that the NAACP was about to reorient itself toward a nonviolent strategy—and promote the mass imprisonment of protesters—were soon dashed. The following day, the national office announced that it had suspended demonstrations in Jackson and the campaign ground to a halt. Wilkins's arrest would mark the height of the national office's foray into the murky world of the jail cell.[56] The following day, conservative leaders were drafted by the national office to take over the movement in Jackson. There was to be no more picketing, no marching, and certainly no more arrests.[57]

The national office's takeover was a bitter blow to the local leadership. Protests had gained strong support from the city's youth. Reverend Edwin King estimated that around five thousand students were ready to fill the jails at this point. "The [students] were ready," he recalled. "This was the last day of classes, we could have filled the jails." Eager to build upon their success, the possibility of inviting Martin Luther King and the SCLC to Jackson had been discussed. According to Edwin King, this threat of "another Birmingham" brought the attention of the federal government. Pressure from Washington had caused the NAACP National Office to intervene.[58] While the murder of Medgar Evers on June 12 temporarily revived the movement, the campaign never recovered. On June 17, NAACP leaders announced that demonstrations had been halted.[59]

Since the NAACP had first confronted the issue of jail-no-bail in 1961, the organization had struggled to resolve the philosophical conflict which it presented. As a result, the national office had walked a tightrope, supplying bail bonds but never actively embracing the principle of arrest and imprisonment as a form of direct protest. The Legal Defense Fund had similarly provided both legal defense and large sums of bail funds to imprisoned civil rights workers. Ironically, it was this very compromise that facilitated the ongoing deployment of jail-no-bail. Throughout the history of the nonviolent movement, very few protesters were truly willing, or able, to remain in jail indefinitely. Without the availability of bail funds to act as a safety net, far fewer people would have entered jail.[60]

Not long after the Jackson protests were brought to a premature end by the national office, officials in both the NAACP and the Legal Defense Fund turned their attention to the ever-increasing demand for bail funds. During September, the national office started negotiations with the National Council of Churches in hopes that it would assume responsibility for the NAACP's bail fund in Mississippi. Two months later, negotiations were underway with a number of organizations for the creation of a National Bail and Appeal Bond Committee. This would be an independent organization which would raise funds and distribute them to any individual involved in civil rights activism in need of bail, regardless of his or her organizational affiliation. The national office observed that the number of arrests that had taken place in 1963 had made it impossible for the national civil rights organizations to meet the demand for bail. The NAACP's plans, however, did not progress quickly. In December 1963, the national office reported it had a total of $268,750 tied up in bail funds, in addition to the thousands of dollars raised locally. By the following March, it was forced to issue a memorandum to state NAACP presidents warning that the demand for bail and appeal bonds was driving the organization into a financial crisis.[61] As civil rights organizations struggled to meet the growing need for bail funds during 1963, thousands of black southerners continued to go to jail.

Student Nonviolent Coordinating Committee workers first arrived in Americus, a town in southwest Georgia close to Albany, in January 1963 to help the already well-established Sumter County Movement.[62] Despite intimidation, early voter registration efforts succeeded in convincing a number of residents to attempt to register to vote. In July, direct-action protests targeted segregation at the local movie theater. In one week, sixty-six students, aged between seventeen and nineteen, were jailed. Protests continued to escalate. On August 8, policemen surrounded a mass march of two hundred and fifty African Americans and started beating them. At some point during the fracas, SNCC field secretaries Donald Harris, Ralph Allen, and John Perdew were arrested and subsequently charged with "attempting to incite insurrection."[63] Nine days later, the same charge was brought against CORE worker Zev Aelony.[64] Under state law, the crime was punishable by death. The following day, a mass march of almost two hundred headed toward the police station in protest of the arrests. Police again intercepted the group, this time using electric cattle prods to attack the marchers before taking them to Sumter County Jail. At this point, with the jails overflowing, authorities passed an ordinance requiring each person to pay an initial fee of $23.50 plus $2 for each day of imprisonment. With the movement in Americus desperately short on funds, this ordinance was a shrewd move by the authorities.[65] As was so often the case, this economic pressure eliminated all but a few Americus adults from the movement, leaving high school and college students to continue the fight.

Included in the hundreds of arrests were thirty-two local girls. The youngest was only nine years old. The few beds in their shared cell were removed, leaving them to sleep on the dirt-covered floor. "The walls were damp and slimy . . . the only time we had light was when the sun shone in," recalled one girl. Their water source was leakage from a broken shower, and it was warm, cloudy, and "tasted rusty." The girls were fed once a day: always four cold, rancid hamburgers. On one occasion a rattlesnake entered the cell. Half an hour after the girls shouted for help, the jailer finally killed it. With Perdew, Harris, Allen, and Aelony in jail, and no assistance available from elsewhere, the girls were held in these conditions for almost a month. Finally, SNCC photographer Danny Lyon managed to take pictures of the girls through the bars of their cell window. They were published in the national media, and the children were released.[66]

While students continued to protest, the four civil rights workers were held on twenty-thousand-dollar bond without a court hearing. It was four weeks before they were brought before a judge. Despite a determined campaign to publicize the plight of these men, three of whom were white Northerners, the national media remained silent about events in Americus. A series of sketches by a German artist, which were published in a number of American newspapers, finally brought national attention to the legal plight of the activists.[67] During their imprisonment, the men were kept in terrible conditions.

Authorities tried to "break" the men by promising early release to anybody who beat them. Exceptionally, every one of the prisoners refused to cooperate. It was not until November 1, three months after they were first arrested, that the case came to court and the statute was declared unconstitutional. Americus officials were no doubt aware that the charges would be defeated. One Americus representative acknowledged that they had used a capital charge against the workers with the intention of "deny[ing] these defendants bond." Despite the organizers' eventual release, the authorities had succeeded in destroying the movement. By early September, without leadership, the direct-action campaign had collapsed.[68] In a letter to Zev Aelony, Gordon Carey argued that events in Americus and elsewhere indicated that times were changing: the segregationists were ready to use the *full* power of the criminal justice system against them. Reflecting upon the significance of this to the future of the movement, Carey contended that the Americus authorities had shown civil rights protesters to be "immature" and "naïve" in their commitment to jail-going. The time had come for them to meet the challenge of spending longer periods of time in jail with "dedication and willingness."[69]

Although some still shared such a sentiment, the reality was often much worse than expected, and many found that their sacrifices failed to bring about any tangible gains. In Plaquemine, Louisiana, CORE had established a vibrant movement by mid-1963. After some success with voter registration, the organization turned to direct action. On August 19, the head of CORE, James Farmer, led more than one thousand protesters to the city jail. In response, police made the first mass arrests in that area to date, with more than two hundred imprisoned, including Farmer. Of all the movement leaders, Farmer was the most committed to the philosophical principles behind jail-no-bail. From a pacifist background, he strongly believed in practicing noncooperation with the white power structure. As a result, he repeatedly refused to accept bail, even though it meant missing the March on Washington.[70] On September 1, 1963, Farmer, now released from jail, led a second mass march of almost nine hundred. Awaiting them at the courthouse were both police and a large mob. The police used tear gas and fire hoses before arresting over four hundred protesters, many of whom were children.[71] Their harsh treatment continued in jail. "Things are pretty unbearable," wrote one high school student. "We can't stand it sure enough since no one has been here to give us an encouraging message. Most of us want out as soon as possible."[72] The treatment of the protesters, just as horrific as that in Birmingham, received scant coverage by the media. News of the demonstrations did, however, draw attention in neighboring Plaquemines Parish. In October 1963, Leander Perez, president of the Plaquemines Parish Council, resolved to devise a jail that would deter even the most committed civil rights worker. Built by the Spanish in 1746, Fort St. Philip was a snake- and mosquito-infested compound, surrounded by marshland and accessible only by boat. This new jail would be reserved exclusively for civil rights "invaders." A few months later, members of CORE were invited on a tour of the facility. This invitation is interesting, for it implies white acknowledgement of the use of jail-no-bail as a tactical response to legal repression. Presumably, Perez hoped that the vile conditions at Fort St. Philip would be enough to deter protests. Such a blatant gesture, however, was hardly necessary. The protesters' jail experiences in Plaquemine had brought a swift end to local activism, and CORE had largely abandoned the area long before the "super prison" was ready.[73] By the end of 1963, Gordon Carey's belief that the movement should once again renew its commitment to longer stays in jail had largely lost support in SNCC, and to a lesser extent within CORE too. Both organizations had established a reputation for working in the most violent and deprived communities. As reflected in Americus, the long-term imprisonment of outside organizers could destroy the momentum they had built up. The idea that one should reject bail and voluntarily languish in a southern jail simply did not make sense within the context of such community organizing efforts. While the jail experience remained a central part of life as a civil rights worker, the idea that one should *choose* to remain in jail no longer fitted with their working conditions.

The year 1963 was the most active for the nonviolent movement, and it brought thousands of protesters into southern jail cells. This included the young and old, the middle and working classes. This was what radical pacifists had longed for when, in 1941, they spoke of the need for an "American Negro Gandhi" to lead his people to jail. Their vision, however, was flawed. King had spoken a lot about jail, and had tried to set an example by refusing bail, but the filling of the jails in protest of unjust laws was not the product of his leadership or any other individual's. When the movement did fill the jails—for it did not happen everywhere—it was due to a combination of grassroots organizing and a shared commitment to challenge the power of the police, judges, and jailers in their own community. These community organizing efforts endured throughout 1963 and onward. However, as the aims, focus, and strategies of civil rights organizing continued to evolve, it became evident that deliberately seeking to fill the jails was difficult, costly, and rarely brought any meaningful change to the treatment of African Americans within a specific locality. It isolated leaders and placed massive pressure upon the rank and file. Nevertheless, the nature of such protests, with their open and direct challenges to white supremacy, made arrest and imprisonment of supporters inevitable. Thus, the importance of the jail experience endured, and the jail cell remained a site of politicization and radicalization. Indeed, in the years to come, its role in radicalizing activists would become ever more important.

5

This Lousy Hole

It was past ten o'clock in the evening of June 21 before James Chaney, Mickey Schwerner, and Andrew Goodman were released from Neshoba County Jail in Philadelphia, Mississippi. Hours earlier, they had been stopped by Deputy Sheriff Cecil Price on the road between Longdale and Meridian and charged with speeding. The three men were part of the 1964 Mississippi Freedom Summer, which was administered by a coalition of the major civil rights organizations working in Mississippi known as the Council of Federated Organizations (COFO). Congress of Racial Equality worker James Chaney was a twenty-one-year-old native of Mississippi. Schwerner, a Jewish New Yorker, had been in Meridian with his wife Rita since January, where he had established a CORE community center. Goodman was one of the many student volunteers who had been recruited to Mississippi for the summer. He had been in Meridian little more than twenty-four hours before he was dispatched alongside Chaney and Schwerner to investigate a church-burning in Longdale. Upon arrest, the men were held in jail and denied their right to make a telephone call. Sheriff Lawrence Rainey ordered their release just after ten o'clock, and the men set off driving back to Meridian in the dark. Before long, they were once again stopped by Cecil Price, but this time he was not alone. Price handed the men over to two carloads of Klan members, who took them down a dirt track. Mickey Schwerner was the first to be shot dead, soon followed by Goodman, and then Chaney. Their bodies were placed in a shallow grave nearby.[1]

For most white Mississippians, the arrival of Freedom Summer volunteers constituted nothing less than an invasion. This was an assault upon their way of life. Harassment, intimidation, violence, and murder were all sanctioned in its defense. The active involvement of local police officers—most notably in the murder of Chaney, Goodman, and Schwerner—served as a vivid reminder of the extent to which legal officials continued to act as guardians of the southern racial order. The Freedom Summer's focus upon voter registration and the establishment of Freedom Schools meant that the traditional cries of "fill the jails" and "jail-no-bail" had no place in the campaign. Volunteers who attended the orientation sessions in Oxford, Ohio, during June were advised to avoid arrest. They could not do their work from a jail cell, and bail would therefore be supplied whenever available. Those organizing the campaign fully expected a barrage of police brutality and arrests on phony charges. At Oxford, COFO representatives tried to prepare the volunteers for the confrontations with police that would inevitably take place through the summer. However, it was clear to them that not all volunteers appreciated the gravity of the situation. Sally Belfrage, who attended the second induction session at Oxford, recalled that one female volunteer asked, "'But you get a chance to go *home* first, don't you? I mean before they take you to jail?' From the lack of reaction, it appeared she was not alone in her illusions."[2] Such naïveté gradually disappeared once the volunteers arrived in Mississippi. Sally Belfrage, assigned to work in Greenwood, recalled, "Every week there were more arrests on sillier charges requiring trips to the police department to bail somebody out. For a while it seemed usually to be George Albertz, a white volunteer whom the police arrested nearly every day for reckless driving, until his car was smashed with bricks one night; then he was arrested for walking, on the charge of 'parading without a permit.'"[3] The local courthouse and jail became familiar places. Whether they were accompanying voter registrants, attending a trial, negotiating bail for a fellow worker, or spending time in jail, activists found the buildings to be vivid reminders of the white power structure's intransigence. "We got used to the policemen's faces, the desk sergeant's stare, the big ledger where the names and charges were inscribed," recalled Belfrage, "and used to waiting, for the judge or Chief Lary or the man with the keys." Behind the desk sergeant, in among the "wanted" bills, the faces of Schwerner, Goodman, and Chaney looked out from the FBI's "missing" poster.[4]

Over one thousand arrests were made during the course of the Freedom Summer. For many volunteers, their first time in jail demonstrated their commitment to the movement, but the heat, hunger, and sheer monotony of incarceration proved deeply stressful. Perhaps worst of all for an individual, however, were the times when he or she was imprisoned alone. The combination of boredom and fear—of never knowing when or how the experience would end—was mentally exhausting. William Hodes described his short period of incarceration during the summer of 1964:

> So there I was: alone in a Southern jail. First thing I did was check the layout of the cell in case I had to protect myself. I pulled the mattresses halfway off the beds so that I wouldn't hit any sharp corners as I went down. . . . I was very jumpy. . . . My pulse was . . . over a hundred the whole three hours I was in jail. . . . Then I was sure they would suddenly drop charges and put me out into the hostile night. That would be really bad, because I knew that trouble was brewing all over the city. . . . Could I hit a cop and get rearrested, or would that beating be worse than the possibility of getting caught by the mob?

I went home to bed, completely exhausted. The mental strain of being in there alone was just too much. While I slept, the office was shot into.[5]

In Natchez, Mississippi, Peter Milenburg, a white Northern college student, described a similar experience in a letter written to friends and family from Adams County Jail. After only five days alone in his cell, Milenburg found himself unable to remember the date and declaring that he would "go crazy" if he had to remain any longer. Already aware that his name was on the Klan's "wanted" list, the news that a group of white men were seeking arrest in order to join him confirmed Milenburg's belief that an attempt might soon be made on his life. In a letter to a friend, written on toilet paper and smuggled out of the jail, Milenburg reflected upon the psychological pressures of incarceration: "I've been in this lousy hole just a couple of hours short of a week, and I think I understand the expression 'stir-crazy.' Sometimes a feeling of desperation wells up in me and I have to force myself to remain calm, to settle my nerves."[6]

Many students came to Mississippi eager to experience jail and imbued with an idealized view of imprisonment as something that would transform them into hardened freedom fighters. Sally Belfrage recalled that going to jail was "a fate almost universally considered desirable" among Freedom Summer volunteers. A woman named Eli claimed: "I want to go to jail. I'm honest. I've never been."[7] Likewise, Milenburg wrote: "Before I ever went to jail I longed for the experience out of curiosity and to put the official stamp on my involvement in the movement." When Milenburg finally went to jail, his enthusiasm soon dissipated. In one of his letters, he wrote:

> Speculating about prison, imagining what it would be like is no substitute for actually experiencing it. It's a lot worse than you imagine. You know beforehand that you're going to feel deprived, cooped up, that you'll want to get out. But once the door clangs harshly shut, the keys jangle in the trustee's hands as he locks the door, the bolt thumps to secure your cell door—well, then you get a more accurate picture of it all.

Take off your shoes and climb into your bunk—there's nothing else to do—lie back. Bars all around and cold steel walls
covered with scratches forming names, obscenities, crude pictures. . . . You lie there blank for a couple of minutes, then sit
up, legs dangling over the bed, looking for something to distract
you. Bars. Faint smell of urine and disinfectant.[8]

The perceptions of jail held by men and women like Milenburg and
Belfrage reveal the extent to which the civil rights jail experience was
shaped by a multitude of factors. Going to jail remained deeply important to the movement as a collective experience, but one's race,
class, age, gender, and place of origin could all shape how one viewed
imprisonment and the treatment one received.

One of the greatest complaints of those women who volunteered
for the Freedom Summer was their assignation to "women's" roles. It
was often expected that they undertake such "housekeeping" chores
as cooking and cleaning, and women were far more likely to be teaching in Freedom Schools than participating in the more dangerous
task of voter registration.[9] One volunteer described feeling "shoved
to the side," while "macho men" faced violence. One must presume,
therefore, that such divisions of duty along gender lines included
an assumption that going to jail was also men's responsibility. If so,
this directly contradicts other examples in the movement. Elsewhere,
women often dominated marches, picket lines, and mass meetings,
and therefore comprised a significant proportion of those incarcerated. One woman in Natchez, Mississippi, complained, "It's these
ladies, people like Mrs. Duncan, Mrs. MacNeilly, Mrs. Muzeek, Mrs.
Jackson . . . they are the people who are really getting the job done
around here." While women "fought off those dogs" and went to jail,
the men took control of the negotiations with city authorities.[10] As
Charles Payne has demonstrated, this tendency of men to dominate
leadership roles within the movement was widespread.[11] Perhaps unsurprisingly, therefore, the suggestion that going to jail was "man's
work" had not been made with any force before the summer of 1964.

Looking at this issue from a wider perspective, however, there can be no doubt that jail was a masculine environment. It held particular significance for black men, as traditionally they had dominated the inmate population and were most likely to experience police brutality. Furthermore, black men were invariably powerless to intervene when their wives or children suffered violence, whether at the hands of police or any other white individual. The celebration of "black bad men" and of violent resistance to police was in direct response to the way in which official violence emasculated black men. The civil rights movement's message of refusing to fear jail no doubt empowered some black men, but the suggestion that they submit to imprisonment and police brutality without resistance was still difficult to accept. This problem was not just restricted to arrest and imprisonment. The movement as a whole sometimes struggled to convince black men that nonviolent resistance could be a "manly" act.[12]

Although some women taking part in the Freedom Summer resented their consignment to teaching, cleaning, and typing, they were certainly not immune from danger. Simply participating in the movement could make one a target for white anger.[13] White Mississippians feared that the Freedom Summer would tear apart the social fabric of the state, and there was no assurance that white women would receive any protection from their venom.

While examples of white women being beaten in jail remained far less common than for white men, this became a greater concern as the movement pushed further into the Deep South. Mary King, arrested and jailed in Atlanta in December 1963, was placed in a cell with a number of other white women, and she resolved not to inform them of her association with the movement. She recalled:

It was common knowledge that white men in the movement were often tossed into white cellblocks specifically for the purpose of provoking violence. . . . Police all over the South knew that a white man in jail for civil rights activities would be beaten and sometimes nearly killed by other whites. . . . Very few white women in the movement had been arrested at that time, however, and there wasn't the same inevitability about our treatment. I didn't know how much we had to fear.[14]

King's reluctance to reveal her identity to her cellmates was well-founded. In February 1964, an eighteen-year-old white woman was badly beaten by other prisoners in Fulton County Jail.[15] For black women, the dangers of jail were even greater.

On June 9, 1963, Fannie Lou Hamer was returning to Mississippi with a number of fellow civil rights activists after attending an SCLC citizenship school in South Carolina. Tired from their journey, they stopped in Winona, Mississippi, to rest. Perhaps inspired by their time in South Carolina, a number of the group sat down at the Trailways bus terminal lunch counter and requested service. As was the case elsewhere, the ICC ruling against segregation of transportation facilities had made no impact, and the group was forced to leave. Once outside, Annelle Ponder, secretary of Greenwood's SCLC chapter, made a point of writing down the license number of one of the patrol cars that had arrived outside the bus terminal. Infuriated, the police officer arrested Ponder, June Johnson, Euvester Simpson, Rosemary Freeman, James West, and Fannie Lou Hamer.

At the county jail, the officers started to beat James West. Next, they turned on Ponder. "I heard her screaming, and they was, you know, beating her," recalled Hamer. "Can't you say 'yes suh' [sic] nigger?" demanded one of the officers. Ponder's response that she did not know the officers well enough only intensified the beating. When Hamer saw Ponder again, "her clothes had been torn from the waste [sic] down, and her mouth was swollen . . . she couldn't see me because . . . they had beat her . . . eyes." Fifteen-year-old June Johnson endured the same torturous ordeal. Finally, three white men came to Fannie Lou Hamer's cell. Hamer's involvement in voter registration had already earned her a reputation as a "troublemaker" in the Delta area. Having discovered the identity of their prisoner, the officers greeted her with the warning, "we going to make you wish you was dead." Hamer was taken into another cell in which waited two African

American prisoners. "That's when . . . they made me lay down on my face, they forced . . . [the prisoners] to beat me." Using a blackjack, one of the prisoners started to beat her back. Hamer used her hands to protect one of her legs, which had been weakened by polio. "They beat me until my hands was navy blue," she recalled. The first inmate, now exhausted, was instructed to pass the blackjack to the second prisoner. "That's when I started screaming and working my feet 'cause I couldn't help it." Angered by her screams, one of the officers "began to beat me about [the] head and told me to stop my screaming. I then began to bury my head in the mattress and hugged it to kill the sound of my screams." The beating left Hamer with a blood clot in her left eye and a permanently damaged kidney; the open wounds on her back took several weeks to heal.[16]

With the attention of reporters friendly to the civil rights movement focused on Tuscaloosa, ready to report on Governor Wallace's famous stand in the schoolhouse door, the arrest and abuse of Hamer and her fellow workers received only scant media coverage. On some occasions, such as in the Freedom Rides and Albany, female civil rights workers received less-harsh treatment from their jailers than their male counterparts, but this was predominantly associated with a desire to avoid negative publicity. With the workers isolated in the county jail, located many miles outside of Winona, there was little such pressure upon the jailers to limit their punishment of Hamer.

The beating of black women by white law officers was a sadly common occurrence in the South. As a child, Robert Williams witnessed the beating of a local black woman by a police officer. He recalled how she was "dragged" back to the jailhouse, her dress over her head, "the same way that a caveman would club and drag his sexual prey."[17] June Johnson endured similar sexual humiliation in Winona Jail when the officers beating her tore off her dress.[18] While the intersection of racial and sexual abuse made black women particularly vulnerable to such treatment, white women were also at risk. Imprisoned women regularly complained that it was rare for the "bathroom" facilities to have any privacy, leaving them fearful to use the toilet or take a shower. Women dreaded the crude and invariably unsanitary internal examinations which sometimes took place upon arrival at jail (and were a particular complaint of female Freedom Riders).[19] Even more serious, however, were complaints of sexual assault. On June 6, 1963, WNEW radio broadcast an interview with Dorothy Height, president of the National Council of Negro Women, in which she reported a secret meeting of individuals concerned with the treatment of imprisoned female civil rights workers. At the meeting, accounts of female activists being raped and abused by southern law officials and jail attendants were given.[20]

In response, the Youth Emergency Fund was established, with its central concern being to pressure the Department of Justice to "assure the personal privacy and protection of girls and women in southern jails." The group mapped out a scheme by which volunteers would visit imprisoned women in order to survey their treatment and the conditions in which they were kept. They also pledged to provide emergency assistance, such as bringing food to the jails.[21] This was the first organized effort concerned specifically with the treatment of female civil rights prisoners. Nine months later, in March 1964, the Inter-Organization Women's Committee met in absolute secrecy at a motel in Atlanta, Georgia. The report from the meeting, which was not made public at the time due to fear of reprisals against those involved, details some horrific treatment of women and girls, both black and white. In particular, a panel of young women recounted for the group their experiences in southern jails. One black woman described her arrest while protesting outside a restaurant in Atlanta. She was taken up to the fifth floor, which was reserved for men, and placed in a cell with some trusties from the jail. The men had been drinking. She and other black women arrested at the same time were sexually assaulted. A sixteen-year-old girl from Albany, Georgia, described to the panel how both she and her thirteen-year-old sister had suffered sexual harassment since they joined the movement. In May 1963, a white SNCC worker reported that she had been molested by police in Albany City Jail. Another white woman suffered similar treatment when she was arrested while handing out voter registration leaflets and taken to Albany City Jail. "We were stripped in view of male prisoners in the cellblock," she described to the *Washington Post*. "The policemen came and stared at us, making insinuations about our morals."[22]

These reports at the Atlanta meeting resulted in the formation of a "ministry of presence" to visit southern jails and prisons and assess the treatment of female inmates. Since the first meeting in 1963, the focus of the group had broadened beyond the treatment of civil rights workers to focus more generally upon the conditions in which all women served time. A charter set out minimum standards for medical treatment, food, sanitation, and the recruitment of guards, and representatives agreed to publicize the need for jail and prison reform in their individual communities and to establish a regular program of visitation to check on inmates.[23] Thus far, civil rights historians have overlooked both the accusations of sexual assault and the campaign to protect female civil rights workers; presumably this is partly a product of the apparent reluctance of those involved—both at the time and subsequently—to openly discuss such events. (Discussion of these experiences is almost nonexistent within oral history testimonies and autobiographical accounts of movement activists.) Such a silence is not surprising, but it is certainly unfortunate; the inclusion of such experiences is important if we are to truly appreciate the risks that women of both races took by joining the movement.[24]

After weeks of voter registration work in Greenwood, registrar Martha Lamb's dogged obstruction brought a decision to picket the courthouse. Sally Belfrage was one of those chosen to join the protest. As predicted, Belfrage and many others were soon placed under arrest and transported to the local jail. The first couple of hours were an "adventure" for Belfrage and her cellmates, but soon the boredom and unbearable heat began to take effect. Crucial help came from a trusty named Patterson. When Belfrage and many of the other volunteers went on a hunger strike, he sneaked candy bars and cigarettes into the cells and passed notes between the various groups spread throughout the building. Without his covert support, their time in jail would have been far harder to bear. It was through Patterson that Belfrage learned firsthand the injustices meted out to African Americans. "Patterson described his case, eighteen-month sentence, innocence," she wrote in *Freedom Summer*. "He explained that as a trusty he lived in an ordinary room, not a cell, and was permitted to go outside at certain hours of the day. . . . The alternative was parole to a farmer, who would 'own me like a slave'; he preferred jail."[25] White, middle-class women like Belfrage were unlikely to have come into contact with the "criminal class" before their own spell in jail. Their incarceration sometimes challenged their views on criminal justice. Mary King, a white SNCC worker imprisoned in Atlanta in December 1963, was shocked to discover that many of the women in jail with her were there for passing bad checks, an offense usually only committed by the poor. "Some of the women with such charges were in difficult circumstances involving the necessity to obtain food or other essentials for their children after having been abandoned." Many of the others were alcoholics. "It began to dawn on me that . . . women incarcerated in jails and prisons at that time were more likely to have been the victims than the perpetrators of violence."[26]

Mary King was not the only activist whose eyes were opened to the nature of the criminal justice system. Dion Diamond, a college-educated black man, was sentenced to two months in Baton Rouge Jail with Ronnie Moore in 1964. During the course of his sentence, he wrote continuously to friends and family describing his time in jail. In one of his first letters, he reflected upon the great gulf between himself and the majority of black prisoners. The "younger prisoners," he wrote, "were gathered around degrading the intelligence of one another . . . the ignorance and lack of raw intelligence was very profound." One letter, written the day of his sentencing, focused upon a fourteen-year-old cellmate named Johnnie. "He found great difficulty," Diamond described, "in comprehending that we worked with whites . . . [he] is a splendid example of how the society here has conditioned the mind and thinking of the Negro . . . with regard to himself. . . . He finds it impossible to accept, as logical, our protest activities. Moreover, whenever he refers to Negroes, he uses the term 'nigger.' I must admit that this word is in common usage around here, and it is used 99% of the time by the inmates."[27] Diamond, like many other activists before him, was left in no doubt about the appalling standard of jail conditions for the general inmate population. Crowded together with 106 other black men in a cell designed for 46, Diamond described these conditions: "5 cells in this block. . . . Each of them ha[ve] mattresses strewn about the floor. If one steps out of his bunk, it is likely that he will place his foot in someone's face. The mattresses have just run out. The men who have just come in are contenting themselves with reclining on the steel tables."[28] Like Sally Belfrage, Diamond was to hear firsthand of the inmates' crimes and of the hypocrisy of southern justice, although he did not always sympathize with their plight. One man had been charged with the rape of a black woman—he had been in jail awaiting trial for five months. His accomplice had entered a guilty plea and was sentenced to one year in the state penitentiary. When the rape of a white woman by a black man was invariably punished by a life term or death, such a short sentence revealed the low value placed on black women by southern courts. The hypocrisy angered Diamond. "The bitterness that I now harbor, and attempt to write with a shaking hand, is directed at the entire white power structures of the world. Better still, at this moment I *hate* any structure which supposedly . . ." At that point, Diamond's epileptic cellmate dropped to the floor in a seizure, hitting his head on a bench as he fell. Diamond broke off his condemnation of worldwide racism to concentrate on trying to get his cellmate medical attention. This had become a regular mission for Diamond, but his appeals to the jailer had so far achieved nothing. The seizing man was dragged over to the front of the cell on a mattress for the jailer to inspect. He "concluded it was nothing serious and ordered him back into the cell."[29]

Over the course of his jail term, Diamond became acquainted with a number of his cellmates—poor, illiterate African Americans who rarely populated the civil rights movement's ranks. When Ronnie Moore was released on March 19, leaving Diamond the only civil rights prisoner in the jail, he resolved to undertake a program of civil rights organizing. In a series of workshops, Diamond sought to educate his cellmates about the movement's work and the importance of self-respect. "[I am] attempting to show them how we can improve ourselves and, at the same time, help to eradicate the stereotype . . . of the Negro."[30] As white authorities inflicted ever-longer jail sentences on civil rights workers, so contact between them and the general inmate population became more common. Due to people like Dion Diamond, black inmates—perhaps the most isolated of all groups in the South—were brought into direct communication with the movement.

As is evident in Diamond's writings, the jail experience had the power to radicalize activists. This is also reflected in a letter written by an unnamed local civil rights leader while he was imprisoned in 1963. Titled "I Only W̶a̶n̶t̶e̶d̶ Want To be Free," it recounts his experience of police arriving at his home in the middle of the night to take him to the county jail.[31] The letter powerfully evokes the fear and anger that often accompanied the jail experience. Like many others before him, he realized that the men taking him from his wife and children at three o'clock in the morning might be planning his murder. After thirty-six hours in a damp and foul-smelling jail cell, he wrote his letter in verse, repeatedly revising it as he pondered why he was incarcerated. The sense of lawlessness and the injustice of the situation—combined with the fear he feels—leads him to question his loyalty to American values.

> I wonder how long the American way of
> life can endure. How long can this so-
> call [sic] Democracy prevail. How much time
> does the Communist need to t̶e̶l̶l̶ ̶t̶h̶e̶ prove to the whole
> world how unjust . . . the A̶m̶e̶r̶i̶c̶
> American way of life is to every m̶a̶n̶ one
> of her c̶o̶l̶o̶r̶e̶d̶ Negro citizens.

Like Dion Diamond, he feels a great distance between himself and his cellmates, but the experience of being treated as a criminal also causes him to rethink his earlier understanding of that term—perhaps his "crime" is not so different from those supposedly committed by the people with whom he shares a cell.

Upon the walls of this cell I see the name
of a Negro that is common to every
[one in town] . . . who
was last arrested for raping one
white woman & murdering another. I
take it, [he] was housed in this
cell. At his trial, they proved he had lived
a lifetime of vitcious crime.
~~(robbery/thief,/cutting & shoot~~
~~ing)~~ Now, I wonder was he guilty? Even if he
executed the acts, who was guilty? Could
~~it have been a case where this man have~~
~~been denied~~ the American way of life
that jailed me because I want to be . . .
free, be guilty. Is it possible for me
to learn to hate the American way
of life and retalliate by trying to
destroy it by crime & violence? Is it
human for a man to protest that
which tries to destroy him?[32]

The civil rights movement had long sought to use the imprisonment of protesters to challenge definitions of "right" and "wrong,"
thereby exposing the hypocrisy of southern justice. This poem, however, explicitly confronts accepted definitions of criminality, suggest-
ing that even a rapist may have been the victim of racist oppression,
as was the author. Such a view would be expressed with greater force
during the late 1960s, as black-power activists looked more closely at
the state of southern jails and prisons.

In September 1964, the Mississippi Freedom Summer finally came
to an end. Robert Moses's grand plan to bring hundreds of Northern volunteers to work in Mississippi may not have burst open the
"closed society," but it had nonetheless exposed it to the scrutiny of
the outside world. Success, however, had come at a high cost. Many
activists in SNCC and CORE who had opposed the recruitment of

white volunteers harbored a deep sense of anger. They had argued that the involvement of outsiders—especially white, middle-class ones—would be fatal to the slow and painstaking work of community organizing for which SNCC and CORE had become famous. By the end of the summer, they believed that their fears had been warranted. The underlying tension between black and white, old and new, had been evident from the beginning. In the fall of 1964 it bubbled to the surface, and this would eventually contribute to SNCC and CORE expelling their white members.[33] Both organizations continued to focus upon voter registration throughout 1964 and 1965. Working in some of the most violent parts of the South, an increasing number of workers started to carry guns. Publicly, they still endorsed nonviolence, but the situation on the ground was more complex. With the nonviolent movement nearing disintegration, the earlier ethos of celebrating the jail experience also disappeared. Indeed, by 1965, the only major civil rights organization which still endorsed filling the jails was the SCLC.

In September 1961, James Lawson, as "special projects director" for the SCLC, had announced preparations to recruit a "nonviolent army" that would be prepared to spend at least six months in jail.[34] The plan never came to fruition, but the bombing of the Sixteenth Street Baptist Church in Birmingham two years later, which killed four young girls, inspired Jim and Diane Bevel to revive the idea. Presented to SCLC headquarters in late September 1963, their proposal aimed to recruit Alabama students and adults to a nonviolent training school in Montgomery, where they would be taught the techniques of civil disobedience. The objective was to remove all impediments to African American voting through the use of nonviolent direct action. This was a strategy that, strictly speaking, had not yet been employed. The Freedom Army was an attempt to restore the original vision of jail-ins as an expression of moral power and brotherly love. "Being in jail can bring about a crisis great enough so that people can not run away from the problem any longer. . . . In this way a freedom army will be of more service to the cause in jail than they could be on the outside," explained the "Freedom Army Handbook." "Each person in jail will have his own moral weight against the unjust government of Alabama," it continued. "As long as he stays in jail he can keep his weight against the state. . . . If our endurance and capacity to suffer are great enough Alabama will have to yield to the weight of righteousness. Alabama will have to let us vote."[35] While SNCC and CORE had largely abandoned their original emphasis upon using jail as a platform for protest, the SCLC appeared to be intensifying its commitment. Ultimately, the Freedom Army did not materialize in the summer of 1964. King, while interested in the idea of the SCLC reentering Alabama, instead decided to focus his attention upon St. Augustine, Florida.

In early 1965, the SCLC finally returned to Alabama after receiving an appeal for help from its affiliate in Selma, the Dallas County Voters League. With its history of racial violence and brutal police chief Jim Clark, Selma seemed an ideal location for the SCLC's long-awaited Alabama campaign. Over one thousand arrests were made during the course of the campaign, including that of King on February 1.[36] Combined with the brutality of Jim Clark's police force and the publicity surrounding the Selma-to-Montgomery march, these arrests helped convince President Johnson that voting legislation had to be placed before Congress.[37] The Selma campaign marked the last time that mass arrests captured the focus of the national mainstream media. By that time, thousands of men and women had spent time inside a southern jail for the cause of civil rights. Collectively, they had taken the battle for racial equality inside one of the most racist and brutal parts of the South, and had made going to jail a central part of the freedom struggle.

The 1964 Freedom Summer was a pivotal time for civil rights activism. The involvement of white volunteers on a scale never seen before, the media attention, the ever-growing dissatisfaction with nonviolence, and the establishment of Freedom Schools brought both new opportunities and challenges to the involved organizations. Despite such developments, as well as the rejection of jail-no-bail, arrest and imprisonment remained a central part of activists' lives. The jail continued to politicize and radicalize those who passed through its cell doors. The process by which this happened was particularly dependent upon the race and gender of the prisoner. White, male civil rights workers generally faced the greatest danger in going to jail. Their interactions with the mainstream inmate population invariably ignited violence and threats; there was little opportunity for them to explore the ways in which the criminal justice system reinforced existing inequalities within the wider society. Dion Diamond's jail letters demonstrate a very different experience. As a black man, he had an opportunity to interact with his fellow inmates. Not only did the experience politicize him, it also apparently politicized some of the inmates with whom he had contact. They may have been unable to escape the physical confines of the jail, but, within their cell, new ideas and exchanges flowed freely. Activists' time in jail often proved eye-opening, making the broader struggle of black prisoners against the brutality and poor conditions of southern prisons a more personal one. It also forced activists to reexamine their assumptions about what constituted criminality. This process gained speed through the mid-1960s as activists faced increasingly severe and destructive criminal charges; physically and morally, this drew them further inside the prison system and focused their attention upon the urgency of reform. It is ironic that the movement of the early 1960s, having filled the jails in protest of conditions on the outside, was never able to protest openly about conditions on the inside. As victims of legal harassment, police brutality, and terrible jail conditions, civil rights workers were constantly aware of the racist nature of the criminal justice system. As a whole, however, the movement was unable to address the plight of "ordinary" prisoners. While there were complaints of police brutality, and demands were sometimes made for more black police officers, protest never went much further. This started to change in the mid-1960s; the battle to improve police-community relations and to bring reform to the southern prison system emerged as a core part of the movement's agenda. The struggle against color-coded justice, having been temporarily sidelined by other issues, once again began to emerge as an important focus of civil rights organizing.

6

You Can't Jail the Revolution

"This is the 27th time I have been arrested—I ain't going to jail no more. I ain't going to jail no more." This was Stokeley Carmichael's message to a rally in Greenwood, held to support the 1966 Meredith March. Earlier in the day, he and two other SNCC workers had been arrested by police as they tried to erect tents on the grounds of a local black high school. That evening, shortly after his release, he told the crowd, "Every courthouse in Mississippi ought to be burned tomorrow to get rid of the dirt."[1] "What do you want?" he asked them. They responded with "black power!" That Carmichael should introduce his call for black power with a reminder of the bigoted nature of the southern criminal justice system is no great surprise. Its failure to punish racist violence—while zealously imprisoning peaceful civil rights protesters—was a painful reminder of just how slowly the

South was changing. In spite of years of exhausting work and the passage of the Civil Rights and Voting Rights Acts, those who challenged white supremacy in the South were still outlaws.

"Black power" was no more a coherent statement of protest philosophy than "freedom now" was in the early 1960s. Both were so popular because they spoke to the aspirations and frustrations of many people. Indeed, black power's popularity lay largely in its malleability. It covered a range of issues and meanings: armed self-defense, political empowerment, economic independence, black separatism, racial pride, and antiwhite sentiment. The speed with which the cry of black power was adopted by SNCC and CORE belied the fact that its underlying ideology had been influencing some activists long before 1966. Racial conflict, vigilante violence, and frustration with the federal government had all taken their toll upon individuals and the movement. The rioting in Northern ghettos from 1964 onward contributed further to the disintegration of the national nonviolent movement by shifting the nation's focus northward, toward the problem of urban poverty. For many members of SNCC and CORE, who had often worked in the most violently repressive parts of the South, the pressure for change—to officially abandon their original philosophy of integration and nonviolence—was great. In 1966, both organizations embraced black power, and SNCC expelled its white members. The same year CORE, facing bankruptcy, closed its southern office. Although it would take a further two years for CORE to officially expel its white members, its black power orientation meant it had few left by that point.[2] The movement's collapse at the national level did not, however, lead to its destruction at the local level. Studies of the movement in Louisiana, North Carolina, and Arkansas demonstrate that community activism continued in many towns and cities.[3] Sometimes, such organizing reflected black power's influence. Lance Hill's study of the Deacons for Defense in Louisiana and Mississippi reveals the extent to which the emphasis upon armed self-defense—in itself not new—was openly embraced by some southern African Americans. Adam Fairclough's study of the movement in Louisiana demonstrates that this heightened commitment to armed self-defense and support for all-black political tickets was evidence of localized support for black power.

Black power supporters focused especially on police brutality during the late 1960s. Numerous confrontations between residents of urban black communities and the police took place, and a number of the most serious riots in Northern cities were sparked by these. Adam Fairclough has suggested that the increased size of the black electorate and the appointment of more black police officers in the South during the late 1960s most likely resulted in an overall reduction in police brutality. The many cries of police brutality during the late 1960s, therefore, reflected "heightened sensitivity" to the issue as a result of riots in the North, as opposed to an increase in the actual levels of violence. While some communities did enjoy a reduction in police brutality, as Fairclough himself observes, many others did not.[4] This was particularly the case in poor, black, urban communities in the South; the civil rights movement had the least impact in these places. Police killings and beatings had long taken place in such communities, and one must question whether it took riots in the North to make residents sensitive to the issue.[5]

By the mid-1960s, SNCC and other black power groups had targeted police brutality as one of the most pressing concerns for black communities. In doing so, they also helped empower those communities most affected by such problems to voice their anger. Carmichael and other militants understood that the police officer was a powerful symbol of American injustice and inequality, whether an individual had suffered brutality at the hands of the police or not. Enmity toward police was compounded by a series of violent confrontations with protesters over the following years. (This was not limited to African Americans: white protesters also became victims of excessive police force when they were perceived to represent a threat to law and order.) Between 1967 and 1972, police fired at protesters on black college campuses in Greensboro, North Carolina; Orangeburg, South Carolina; Jackson, Mississippi; and Baton Rouge, Louisiana.

While black power greatly appealed to southern African Americans, it did not wipe out the legacy of the preceding decade. The vacuum created by the withdrawal of SNCC and CORE from the South enabled the NAACP to regain support. Now more radical and open to nonviolent protest, it offered communities an alternative to black power. Outside assistance was also available from the Southern Regional Council, Voter Education Project, and the federal government, particularly from Johnson's War on Poverty programs.[6] In some places, the established tactics of protest marches, mass meetings, and jail-ins persisted. David Cecelski's study of school desegregation in Hyde County, North Carolina, reveals the continued use of nonviolent protest in the late 1960s. In 1968, the local community received assistance from the SCLC in organizing a school boycott to protest the planned closure of two local black schools. When local youths held a sit-in at an office on the second floor of the Hyde County Courthouse, police fired tear gas grenades inside and then held the door of the building shut. In the rush for fresh air, a seventeen-year-old girl fell from a window, breaking her pelvis. The protest leadership, aware of just how angry local residents were at the children's treatment, planned a series of protest marches. With the local jail overflowing, authorities were forced to dispatch the inmates throughout the surrounding counties. Once again, the cry of "fill the jails" was heard.[7]

Although the jail-in was evidently still in use during the late 1960s, for the most part, the idea that one could bring about change via mass imprisonment no longer appeared realistic or relevant to the attainment of such key goals as black political influence and unity. Nevertheless, authorities continued to legally repress racial "agitators." In some of the most oppressive places, the police harassed and intimidated anybody who dared to challenge the racial status quo, but those who associated with black power organizations became the central focus of these tactics. The racial separatism, antiwhite rhetoric, and use of self-defense advocated by some activists elicited an almost hysterical reaction from many whites, who were terrified by the prospect of black revolutionaries like Carmichael touring the nation and stirring up racial violence. With the rioting in Northern ghettos worsening by the year, such fears were apparently confirmed. The sense that the nation was under siege by a variety of extremist groups, bent on revolution, came to the fore with the election of Richard Nixon in 1968 on a platform of law and order. That same year, J. Edgar Hoover expanded the FBI's counterintelligence program (COINTELPRO) to include "Black Nationalist-Hate Groups," and authorized agents to disrupt the growth of such organizations.[8] During the early 1960s, attempts to destroy the civil rights movement through the courts had relied upon the efforts of the local sheriff and jailer. The FBI, already a focus of anger due to its refusal to investigate cases of violence against civil rights workers, now became a central player in the campaign to crush black power organizations. As had been the case earlier in the decade, illegal searches, arrests, and convictions associated with the FBI's campaign absorbed funds and undermined organizing efforts. In contrast to the early 1960s, when individuals were often held in jail for a matter of days on such charges as vagrancy and loitering, black power activists faced decades in prison on felony charges, including murder. The movement was limited in its responses: proving that such charges were politically motivated now presented a far greater challenge. Black power advocates faced increasingly organized and efficient law enforcement, which used paid informants and witnesses to build an apparently airtight case against them. Furthermore, black power's advocacy of armed self-defense and violent rhetoric, as well as the involvement of some associated individuals in genuinely illegal activity, made such charges appear credible to outside observers (who were already rattled by news reports of riots and the breakdown of law and order). The remainder of this chapter surveys how local and state law enforcement, sometimes with the help of the FBI, undermined the organizing efforts of black power groups in three southern communities.

In Birmingham, Alabama, the Alabama Black Liberation Front (ABLF), a group close to the Black Panther Party (BPP), had caught the attention of local authorities by 1971. On September 15, Ronald Williams and Weyland "Doc" Bryant were at the home of Mrs. Bessie Turner, a seventy-year-old woman, in Tarrant City, Alabama. The previous day she had received an eviction notice due to nonpayment of her mortgage, and had asked for the ABLF's assistance. With help from a local black businessman, the eviction was delayed for a further three days. While Turner was at work, Bryant, Williams, Harold Robertson, Robert Jakes, and Brenda Griffin, all members of the ABLF, remained at the property and set about discussing ways to raise funds. That afternoon, members of the Jefferson County Sheriff's Department arrived at Turner's home and arrested its five occupants. Griffin and Jakes were released, but Bryant, Williams, and Robertson were charged with assault with intent to murder and held on twenty-thousand-dollar bonds. A month later, a preliminary hearing ordered Robertson's extradition to New York to face charges of third-degree attempted burglary. The other two were charged with assaulting a police officer with a deadly instrument, a 1967 statute which carried a penalty of two to twenty years. A year later both men were found guilty.[9]

The Republic of New Afrika (RNA) became the target of local law enforcement and the Jackson Division of the FBI when the organization, committed to the foundation of a separate black nation in Mississippi, almost succeeded in buying a large plot of land in the state in 1970. Authorities successfully frustrated further attempts to secure land, and were soon committed to the organization's outright destruction. Imari Obadele, RNA's leader, became the focus of the campaign. "If Obadele can be kept off the streets," noted a memo from law enforcement agencies, "it may prevent further problems involving the RNA."[10] On August 18, 1971, police officers and FBI agents launched simultaneous raids upon the Jackson, Mississippi, headquarters of the RNA and upon Obadele's home. The occupants were given seventy-five seconds' warning before police opened fire on the house. In the gunfight that ensued, a police officer was killed. A total of eight men and three women, including Obadele, were arrested during the raids. They were charged with a range of offenses, including assault, murder, and waging war on the state of Mississippi.[11]

In North Carolina, a state which prided itself on being a symbol of the "New" South, local and state authorities launched a sustained attack upon black power through the courts. Christopher Schutz has documented the case of the Charlotte Three, in which alleged "black militants" James Grant, Charles Parker, and T. J. Reddy were found guilty of unlawful burning in connection with a blaze at the Lazy B. Stables in Charlotte on September 24, 1968. Almost a year earlier, Reddy had visited the stables with his white girlfriend. The owner, Bill Medlin, refused Reddy's request to rent a horse for the afternoon. The following day, Reddy returned to the stables, accompanied by friends, and Medlin allowed him to ride. The case remained open until, three years later, Reddy and his friends were indicted for the barn burning.[12] According to authorities, they had burnt the barn in retaliation for the owners' refusal to allow Reddy to rent a horse. All three were well-known for their involvement in organizing the local black community. They had been members of the local Black Cultural Association (BCA), which attracted a number of black power supporters with its demands for housing reform, economic empowerment of black communities, and the teaching of black history in schools. Walter Washington and Theodore Hood had also been involved with the BCA, and both had long criminal records. In exchange for statements implicating the three men in connection with the barn burning, Hood and Washington were each granted immunity from prosecution and paid at least four thousand dollars. On the basis of these uncorroborated statements, Reddy, Grant, and Parker were found guilty of the charges in July 1972. Parker was sentenced to ten years, Reddy to twenty, and Grant to twenty-five.[13]

These are but a few examples of how black power activists in southern towns and cities disappeared inside jails and prisons. Starting in 1968, the Black Panther Party, responding to the incarceration of so many of its members, had started to label them "political prisoners" and "prisoners of war." The language fitted perfectly with the Panthers' well-established vendetta against the police, whom the party perceived to be an "occupying force" within black neighborhoods.[14] As the Black Panther Party struggled to free its incarcerated members, so the conditions inside America's jails and prisons attracted greater attention. The *Black Panther* began to publish regular reports and letters from imprisoned members on the racist, brutal treatment of black inmates. For example, in August 1969, the party's newspaper contained a detailed description of the treatment of black inmates in New York City Jail, known as the "Tombs," where three of the New York Twenty-One were being held.[15] Although this interest in prison activism was most evident within the Black Panther Party, and particularly in California, similar developments also took place in the South. In North Carolina, supporters of the Charlotte Three soon rallied to their cause, forming the North Carolina Political Prisoners Committee (NCPPC). In Birmingham, the Concerned Citizens for Justice and Urgent Inc. were founded to fight the convictions of Bryant and Williams and to coordinate fund-raising efforts within the local community. The NCPPC's first task was to raise the mammoth $125,000 bonds placed on the defendants while their appeals were made. This was made even harder when the court demanded the full amount in cash, refusing to follow the convention of accepting ten percent through a bail bonding company. The NCPPC worked hard to keep the case in the media spotlight. It started producing newsletters, mailing them to supporters both inside and outside the state, while also making fund-raising appeals. North Carolina Political Prisoners Committee newsletters also looked beyond specific attempts to crush black power to discussion about the prison system more generally. In one edition, Jim Grant described conditions inside Mecklenburg County Jail: sixteen prisoners lived in a cell twenty-four feet wide by forty feet long, which was divided into living and eating areas by sliding doors. Health care had not improved since the mid-1960s, when Dion Diamond tried unsuccessfully to secure medical attention for his epileptic cellmate. The food was inadequate; cells were dirty and ridden with cockroaches and other vermin.[16]

Jails and prisons continued to act as a moral, physical, and psychological battleground between activists and the white power structure. There was never any possibility that black power activists would flood the jails and prisons, but, without the pressures of "respectability" and integration felt by the nonviolent movement, they were free to tackle such "thorny" issues as black criminality and prison reform. By 1970, the Black Panther Party had established itself at the front line of the campaign for penal reform, hoping to eliminate brutal and racist treatment of black inmates. This was most evident in California, where Panthers were heavily involved in a radical prison rights movement that had emerged within Soledad, San Quentin, and Folsom prisons.[17] By 1970, such demands for prison reform, combined with the incarceration of hundreds of Panthers across the nation, resulted in the organization adopting a more radical definition of what constituted a "political prisoner." This broadened perspective viewed many poor and black inmates as political prisoners "in the sense that they are largely victims of an oppressive politico-economic order."[18] As the BPP focused upon fighting the imprisonment of its members, so these ideas became increasingly influential upon it. Cofounder Huey Newton recalled how his incarceration made him "aware that for Black People in particular and poor people in general, the prison is simply a more distinctive form of entrapment within the massive walls of exploitation which is our experience in the United States."[19] There is evidence that this concept also influenced the campaigns to free imprisoned activists in the South. For example, in Birmingham, a newsletter supporting Bryant and Williams claimed: "So that you can understand the POW's problems that are in Viet Nam then you should recognize the POW's in your backyard. . . . Each prisoner is a captured victim of the war of survival." Likewise, in Charlotte, a letter from Parker, printed in the NCPPC newsletter, stated:

> One cannot overlook or refuse to acknowledge the link between the people of the oppressed races in this country and the political prisoners. . . . There are those who are opposed to and struggle against the oppressive and atrocious conditions that this capitalist system thrives on. They are the victims of political frame-ups. There also exist those prisoners who may or may not be political people at first. But, while in prison, they become victims of political indignations and repression.[20]

This argument—that all nonwhite prisoners were, at some level, victims of a racist criminal justice system—powerfully appealed to many members of poor, urban, black communities, as well as the black inmate population in general.[21] Prison authorities had even greater reason to fear the spread of such ideas to the prison population at large than had jailers during the early 1960s. The prison was increasingly viewed as a "breeding ground" for revolutionaries by black and white radicals alike, and the black prisoner was often held up as an idealized symbol of the absolute inequality and injustice of American society.[22]

The Black Panther Party was undoubtedly the most successful of all black power groups at infiltrating and influencing black prisoners. Again, this was particularly the case in California and New York, but there is also evidence of southern activities. On July 26, 1971, inmates in New Orleans Parish Prison launched a boycott of court appearances. They demanded the resignation of District Attorney Jim Garrison, whom the inmates perceived as the "ringleader" of a cruel and inhuman prison system. Their grievances focused upon unfair sentencing and poor living conditions in the prison. Inmates' demands included adequate legal representation, improvements in living conditions, a law library, advancements in medical care, and the lowering of prices at the commissary wagon from which prisoners bought basic supplies. The protest was engineered by black inmates, although their complaints related to the treatment of all prisoners. It was no coincidence that twenty-four members of the New Orleans Black Panther Party were being held in the prison in connection with a series of police raids on their headquarters the previous fall.[23] The party's influence was evident in the inmates' demands, which had been written in the form of a Panther-style "Ten-Point Program."[24] Robert King Wilkerson arrived at the prison in November 1971. He recalled that they had no problems communicating with Panthers held there, who organized political education classes. Two BPP members, Shelly Batiste and Ronald Ailsworth, were held on the same tier as Wilkerson, where conditions were terrible: "filthy mattresses, roaches three inches long, biggest you ever saw a roach, rats." In protest, the Panthers helped organize a hunger strike.[25]

It was not only advocates of black power, however, who had begun to express an interest in prison reform. The rhetoric of law and order during the late 1960s and 1970s had drawn attention to the operation of the police, courts, and prisons among a number of civil rights groups. By the early 1970s, the plight of black prisoners had become a pressing concern not just among black power supporters, but also within the civil rights struggle more generally. David Rothman has observed that many of the lawyers who worked on prisoners' rights in the late 1960s and early 1970s had first become involved in prison reform as a result of representing imprisoned civil rights workers. They effectively "follow[ed] their clients in jail."[26] The NAACP Legal Defense Fund's action concerning the treatment of Freedom Riders in Parchman Farm is one of the best, and earliest, examples of how the movement contributed indirectly to prison reform. By the end of the decade, the Fund had targeted a range of racial issues in the criminal justice system, including the use of the death penalty to punish rape, the desegregation of prisons and jails, and the punishment of inmates. Exploiting the movement's legislative victories of the 1950s and 1960s, civil rights lawyers tackled the South's prison system. For example, in 1970, a federal district judge ordered the reform of the entire penal system in Arkansas. By the mid-1970s, the very worst abuses in southern prisons and jails were disappearing.[27]

No other case demonstrated civil rights organizations' interest in penal conditions more clearly than that of Joan Little. On the night of August 27, 1974, Little was sleeping in her cell in Beaufort County Jail in Washington, North Carolina. This had been her home for the last three months, while she awaited her appeal hearing on a conviction of breaking and entering. Little was the only female prisoner in the jail that evening. (This was not unusual in such a small facility.) While a female matron remained on duty during the day, only male jailers were present during the evening. In the early hours of the morning, jailer Clarence Alligood stood outside Little's cell. He removed his shoes, walked in, and started to strip. Wearing only a shirt and carrying an ice pick in his left hand, Alligood approached Little. Pulling her to the ground, he forced Little to perform oral sex. She tried to grab the ice pick, and a struggle ensued between the large jailer and 5' 3" Little. Joan Little ran from her cell after stabbing Alligood eleven times with the pick. One of these strikes had punctured his heart and another had hit his right temple. Little got dressed and ran from the jail, heading to her home on Pierce Street, where her cousin Jerome was living. He refused to take her in. Little fled along Seventh Street, where Ernest Barnes, sitting outside his house at the time, offered for her to stay with him. Meanwhile, Alligood's body had been found in the cell. A murder investigation was launched, with Little as the only suspect. The local media immediately mourned the passing of a good man who died in the course of serving his community. The fact that his body had been found partially naked, with Little's nightwear close by and semen on his inside thigh, was not mentioned. Instead, Little was portrayed as a violent murderer, and local white men clamored to assist the police in hunting her down. Barnes continued to shelter Little, hiding her under a feather mattress on the four occasions that police arrived at his home with rifles to search for her. Recognizing that her life would be in danger if she were captured by local law enforcement, Little decided she should surrender to the state. A local woman, Marjorie Wright, had tracked Little down and now set about helping her surrender. Wright was in contact with SCLC lawyer Jerry Paul and local civil rights activist Golden Frinks. Wright drove Little, wearing a wig, to a prearranged meeting with Jerry Paul. Over the course of the next few days, Paul made arrangements with the State Bureau of Investigation for her surrender. On September 9, Joan Little was charged with first-degree murder, with the associated threat of the death penalty.[28]

Meanwhile, Little's case had attracted the attention of organizations interested in a range of causes: women's rights, prisoners' rights, and civil rights. Before long, a Joan Little Defense Committee was formed, with the SCLC, Southern Poverty Law Center, National Organization of Women, NAACP, and Black Panther Party all expressing their interest in Little's fate. Little was held without bond and in solitary confinement at the Raleigh Women's Prison for six months, until, with the help of the Southern Poverty Law Center, enough funds had been raised to cover her bail. She was released on bond in March 1975, and was finally brought to trial the following August, by which time a total of two hundred thousand dollars had been donated by the public to support her defense.[29] The trial that summer captured nationwide attention: her case not only raised the question of a woman's right to defend herself against rape, it also highlighted the inadequate provisions for female inmates, and, in some measure, decided whether southern justice had finally escaped its long history of racism. The not-guilty verdict on August 15 was celebrated as a great victory by all those involved in her defense. Little's case had marked a turning point for civil rights organizations. Frinks recalled, "it was the first time I could remember when a civil-rights organization went out on a case, where murder was the spark. . . . It was a brand-new area of civil rights."[30]

Little's case ended just as questions were being raised in the state over the convictions of the Charlotte Three. Details of the FBI's involvement in the cases, as well as payments made to the witnesses, had been revealed in a series of newspaper articles. The campaign to reverse the convictions gained strength, and all three men were eventually released during the late 1970s. In the meantime, however, the legal assault upon black militancy in the city had been effective in isolating and undermining those who had sought to organize the local black community.[31]

These accounts represent just a few of the many campaigns launched against alleged black militants in communities across the South. As is evident in Charlotte, Birmingham, and New Orleans, those incarcerated as a result of their activism did not abandon their struggle against the white power structure. Instead, they continued their battle inside the prisons, seeking to politicize their fellow black inmates. While they achieved some success in this, it was little compensation for the way in which their lives—and their organizing efforts—had been destroyed by local, state, and federal law enforcement agencies. White authorities may not have been able to jail the revolution, but they could certainly jail revolutionaries.

As historians have observed in recent years, the shift from civil rights to black power was not as sudden as has been suggested; it was a far more gradual and complex process than has been traditionally portrayed.[32] The same was true with the role of arrest and imprisonment. Activists increasingly identified with the mainstream inmate population, and sought to use their organizing skills to bring some relief from the dehumanizing, brutal treatment they often suffered. This represented a merging of activist and prisoner identities, such that the black prisoner came to be viewed as the natural inheritor of the revolutionary spirit. We can see this process in action from at least 1963 as activists from within SNCC and CORE, in particular, adopted a more radical agenda and consequently faced increasingly serious criminal charges. They built upon the realization that imprisonment was a strong politicizing experience and that the criminal justice system was a powerful enemy of racial advancement. Civil rights activists constantly fought against the criminalization of their activities. This same battle had been fought in the 1940s, 1950s, and 1960s. Although the setting and tactics may have changed, the essence of the movement's response remained the same. They sought to turn the jail from a site of racial control to one of psychological liberation; from something to be feared to something to be celebrated. It was a difficult, dangerous, and painful battle, but one that had to be fought if they were to ever bring meaningful and long-lasting change to the South.

Conclusion

The criminal justice system had been a source of frustration and anger to southern African Americans long before the civil rights protests of the 1960s. The movement's responses to arrest and imprisonment were, ultimately, rooted in this history. By making the jail cell an ideological and physical battleground, activists not only targeted a stronghold of white supremacy, they also directly challenged white definitions of "right" and "wrong." Large numbers of African Americans came to perceive imprisonment as a white supremacist political act, one which had the potential to control and intimidate those who threatened white authority. As Michael Foucault has argued, prison is traditionally a place where criminals—those ostensibly without a sense of morality—are shut away from the rest of society.[1] By linking the cause of the freedom struggle with jail, African American protesters sought to challenge not only their imprisonment, but also the moral validity of the society that judged them "criminal."

The struggle to take metaphorical control of the jail was one that involved redefining mainstream understandings of freedom and criminality; it was a battle between the jail as a site of repression and a site of liberation. One should not underestimate the difficulties of such a transformation. For decades, activists had sought to keep African Americans out of prison and jail; now, some of them were arguing that blacks should instead *seek out* arrest and imprisonment, and do everything they could to *remain* in jail. We can see evidence of such changing attitudes from the mid-1950s, as reflected in the Montgomery Bus Boycott. Crucially, however, ideas about how to challenge the legal repression of civil rights activism often remained grounded in a concern for respectability, a phenomenon that was especially strong within the black middle classes that invariably dominated the ranks of those organizing civil rights protest. They were willing to accept arrest and imprisonment, and refused to be intimidated by threats of criminal charges. However, it did not make sense to go any further, especially with the NAACP's ongoing dominance.

As civil rights activism expanded and developed its strategies and targets throughout the 1960s, so the role of arrest and imprisonment changed, responding to a multitude of factors that are evident throughout this study. Most important, this dynamic process was shaped by organizational policy and competition between the national groups, the personal experiences of incarcerated activists, and the attitudes and strategies of their segregationist opponents.

Each of the four national civil rights organizations had their own policies governing how their supporters should respond to arrest and imprisonment. (However, on the ground, local conditions were equally important in shaping responses to mass arrest and imprisonment.) Such policies generated considerable intraorganizational conflict. This was most obviously the case with the NAACP, which perceived the idea of jail-no-bail as both dangerous and counterproductive. Despite enthusiastic proclamations from SNCC, CORE, and SCLC that jail-no-bail stood at the center of their response to mass arrest, the reality was often far more complicated. Beyond the campaigns that attracted national attention, it was relatively uncommon to choose to remain in jail. Rather, lack of bail funds most often kept activists incarcerated. While the celebration of jail-going was widespread, and individuals were encouraged to reject bail wherever possible, criminal charges were often challenged in court. The NAACP played an important role in supplying both bail funds and legal assistance in this respect.[2] For those most ideologically committed to nonviolence, such compromise was deeply troubling. From late 1960 right through to 1965, there was ongoing debate over whether such cooperation with legal authorities represented a failure of the nonviolent movement. The jail-ins of 1961 reflected the height of a belief that one could transform the South via mass imprisonment. By the following year, this perspective had already lost influence. Although attempts to fill the jails continued to take place, most especially within the SCLC, the greater use of community organizing made it even harder to persuade large numbers of people to go to jail and stay there. By 1964, activists were facing increasingly serious charges, and only the SCLC still embraced the jail-in as a crucial weapon in its campaign for change.

A second theme that can be drawn from this study is the way in which going to jail was often a transformative experience. This transformation was shaped by a multitude of factors, although one's race, class, and gender were especially important in determining the treatment one received from legal authorities and cellmates. For every imprisonment, there is a story of how it affected the individual and their family and friends.

Thirdly, the jail experience's ability to politicize and radicalize those involved influenced both individuals and the development of protest strategy and focus. For some, going to jail marked a turning point in their commitment to racial change and drew them further into the movement. Others quickly learned that "criminals" could also be victims of a legal system that reinforced prevailing racial, gender, and class prejudices. They found that the experience challenged their assumptions about who went to jail, and why. Their interactions with the mainstream prison population personalized the struggle against unequal justice, and, if only temporarily, pushed prison reform to the front of their minds. The relations between these two groups played an important role in pushing the civil rights movement as a whole toward embracing penal reform as a central part of its agenda.

Finally, this entire history was the product of white communities' determination to maintain a system of racial apartheid, even if it meant appropriating all the machinery of the criminal justice system to do so. It proved an incredibly effective tool for white segregationists, but activists fought long and hard to resist their efforts to suppress protest. Ultimately, this battle helped push civil rights groups to challenge some of the most cruel, brutal, and racist practices of southern life.

On April 18, 2006, the Alabama legislature voted unanimously to pass a bill, dubbed the Rosa Parks Act, that pardoned all civil rights activists who still had a criminal record in connection with protests against Jim Crow segregation. The act not only pardoned such well-known figures as Rosa Parks and Martin Luther King Jr., it also applied to hundreds of other convictions dating back to the early 1900s. The news brought mixed emotions. For some, it was a long-overdue recognition of their unjust treatment.[3] Others, however, were troubled by the idea of being "pardoned," arguing that they had never committed a crime in the first place. Either way, they had lived for decades with criminal records, and some had struggled to find employment or secure a mortgage as a result. No matter how much the movement celebrated going to jail, the efforts of white authorities to crush civil rights organizing through arrest and imprisonment were deeply destructive. A reminder of just how destructive came the following month, when the *Clarion-Ledger* reported that Mississippi governor Haley Barbour had announced he would not issue a posthumous pardon to Clyde Kennard.[4] Five months earlier, Johnny Lee Roberts, who had been a key witness in Kennard's 1960 burglary trial, finally spoke publicly about the case. Roberts was a victim of the case too: he had been forced to testify against a man he deeply respected.

"With somebody like me," Roberts recently stated, "I couldn't control nothing back then. . . . Why they got him was not the feed. . . . If he wasn't a black man trying to go to Southern, you wouldn't have heard nothing."[5] In recent years, the battle to convict those who murdered and maimed individuals in the fight to maintain white supremacy has finally started to bear fruit. Not until there is full recognition of the many lives that were also destroyed by the criminalization of civil rights activity will justice finally be served.

Notes

Introduction

1. Hampton and Fayer, eds., *Voices of Freedom*, 102.

2. O'Brien, *The Color of the Law*.

3. For more on the postbellum development of the southern criminal justice system as a form of racial control, see Ayers, *Vengeance and Justice*; Carleton, *Politics and Punishment*; Curtin, *Black Prisoners*; McMillen, *Dark Journey*; Miller, *Crime, Sexual Violence*; Oshinsky, *Worse than Slavery*; Taylor, *Down on Parchman Farm*.

4. Fairclough, *Race and Democracy*, 88–98.

5. The most comprehensive studies of this subject to date include Carson, *In Struggle*; King, *Civil Rights and the Idea of Freedom*; Garrow, *Bearing the Cross*; Meier and Rudwick, *CORE*. They do not, however, share the aim of this study, which is to place arrest and imprisonment at the forefront of civil rights history.

6. Ayers, *Vengeance and Justice*; Curtin, *Black Prisoners*; O'Brien, *The Color of the Law*.

7. Hampton and Fayer, eds., *Voices of Freedom*, 102.

8. Watters, *Down to Now*, 114.

9. Payne, "Men Led, but Women Organized," 1–4.

10. Fairclough, *Race and Democracy*, xiv–xv.

11. See, for example, Lewis, *Massive Resistance*.

12. Hampton and Fayer, eds., *Voices of Freedom*, 102.

Chapter 1. An American Negro Gandhi?

1. Smith, "Report of the Secretary of Committee on Non-Violent Techniques," March 28–May 25, 1941, box 3, FOR. See also Wittner, *Rebels Against War*.

2. "NVDA Committee Minutes," February 15, 1945, box 4, FOR; Farmer, "The Coming Revolt Against Jim Crow," *Fellowship*, May 1945; Meier and Rudwick, *CORE*, 8. "Minutes of Racial and Industrial Department," September 17, 1946, box 4, FOR; "Minutes of Racial and Industrial Committee Meeting," March 13, 1947, box 4, FOR; Arsenault, *Freedom Riders*, 11–55; Barnes, *Journey from Jim Crow*, 59–60; Meier and Rudwick, *CORE*, 34–39.

3. Meier and Rudwick, "The Origins of Nonviolent Direct Action," 348; Du Bois, "As the Crow Flies," *New York Amsterdam News*, March 13, 1943. For more information on CORE during the 1940s, see Meier and Rudwick, *CORE*, 23–24.

4. Meier and Rudwick, "The Origins of Nonviolent Direct Action," 363–65; Hill, *The Deacons for Defense*; Tyson, *Radio Free Dixie*.

5. Kelley, "'We Are Not What We Seem,'" 75–112.

6. Parks, *Rosa Parks*, 116.

7. Ibid., 118–23.

8. Raines, *My Soul Is Rested*, 40; interview with Rosa Parks, CRDP.

9. Parks, *Rosa Parks*, 113–26.

10. Banks, "Trailblazers: Women in the Montgomery Bus Boycott," 78.

11. Raines, *My Soul Is Rested*, 37.

12. Ibid., 46–47.

13. Gibson, *The Montgomery Bus Boycott*, 37–38.

14. Ibid.

15. Tyson, "Robert F. Williams," 1.

16. Branch, *Parting the Waters*, 160–61.

17. Carson, ed., *Papers of Martin Luther King*, vol. 3, 114.

18. Abernathy, *And the Walls*, 166–67.

19. Ibid., 168–69.

20. On radical pacifism, see Sibley and Jacob, *Conscription of Conscience*; Katz, "Radical Pacifism and the Contemporary Peace Movement," PhD Diss.; Tracy, "Forging Dissent in an Age of Consensus," PhD Diss.

21. Letter from Al Hassler to Glenn Smiley, November 5, 1955, box 9, FOR.

22. Tracy, "Forging Dissent in an Age of Consensus," 158.

23. See Fairclough, *To Redeem the Soul*, 42–44, 54.

24. Watters, *Down to Now*, 124.

25. See "Memorandum to Governor J. P. Coleman" from Zak Van Landingham, September 21, 1959, file 1–27, MSSC. See also "How Mississippi Southern Stayed White. The Story of Clyde Kennard," n.d., reel 7, SNCC; Dittmer, *Local People*, 79–83; Evers, *For Us the Living*, 214–23; Oshinsky, *Worse than Slavery*, 231–33.

26. Bennett, *What Manner of Man*, 98.

Chapter 2. Jail-No-Bail!

1. "Now it is a nice thing to go to jail," *Afro-American*, March 5, 1960, 5.

2. Chafe, *Civilities and Civil Rights*, 118.

3. "Negro Sitdowns Stir Fear of Wider Unrest in South," *New York Times*, February 16, 1960, 1; "Here's Why South Couldn't Stop Sitdowns," *Afro-American*, February 4, 1961, 8. See also Carson, *In Struggle*, 11.

4. "Sitdown Arrests Unlawful," *Afro-American*, March 5, 1960, 1.

5. Interview with Dion T. Diamond, CRDP; letter from James Robinson, May 6, 1959, reel 19, CORE; letter to Gordon Carey from James Farmer, September 30, 1959, reel 19, CORE; letter to John Brown from Gordon Carey, October 16, 1959, reel 19, CORE; Morris, *The Origins*, 198.

6. Wolff, *Lunch at the 5 & 10*, 101.

7. Chafe, *Civilities and Civil Rights*, 137.

8. Lewis, *Massive Resistance*.

9. Fairclough, *Race and Democracy*, 271–72; Lewis, *Massive Resistance*, 135.

10. "A chronological listing of the cities in which demonstrations have occurred," box 289, part 3, NAACP-LOC; "'. . . And the Voice of the Student Shall Be Heard Through the Land,'" *Afro-American*, May 14, 1960, 4–5.

11. "Negro Sitdowns Stir Fear of Wider Unrest in South," *New York Times*, February 16, 1960, 1; "Here's Why South Couldn't Stop Sitdowns," *Afro-American*, February 4, 1961, 8. See also Carson, *In Struggle*, 11.

12. "'Sit-Ins' Vow To Go To Jail For Justice," *Afro-American*, February 27, 1960, 5; "King Lauds Group For Sit-Down Act," *Chicago Defender*, February 27, 1960, 12.

13. As Taylor Branch observes, "fill the jails" was a new "battle cry" for King. See *Parting the Waters*, 276. "'Fight Will Continue' Dr. King," *Afro-American*,

February 27, 1960, 1; "A Creative Protest," *Chicago Defender*, February 16, 1960, 5; Carson et al., eds., *The Papers of Martin Luther King, vol. 5*, 367–70.

14. "Civil Liberties Docket," <http://sunsite.berkeley.edu/meiklejohn/meik-5_3/>, accessed July 31, 2005.

15. Fairclough, *To Redeem the Soul*, 53–54.

16. See Carson, *In Struggle*, 13–14. The *Afro-American* estimated that 240 protesters had been arrested, see "Sitdown Arrests Unlawful. Trials for 110 Scheduled In Four Cities This Week," March 5, 1960, 1.

17. "'We're Not Stopping,' Says Youth," *Afro-American*, March 5, 1960, 1.

18. "A Weapon for the Strong and Brave," *Afro-American*, February 27, 1960, 1; "It's Worth Going to Jail For," *Afro-American*, March 19, 1960, 4; "Now it is a nice thing to go to jail," *Afro-American*, March 5, 1960, 5.

19. "Now it is a nice thing to go to jail," *Afro-American*, March 5, 1960, 5.

20. King, *Civil Rights and the Idea of Freedom*.

21. "Report of Student Protest," April 9, 1956, box E15, part 3, NAACP-LOC.

22. See Oppenheimer, *The Sit-In Movement*, 168–73; Zinn, *SNCC*, 24–25.

23. "Memorandum on sit-down demonstrations in South Carolina by Reverend C. Ivory," n.d., reel 10, part 20, NAACP. See also Oppenheimer, *The Sit-In Movement*, 168–73; Zinn, *SNCC*, 24–25.

24. "Memorandum," n.d., reel 10, part 20, NAACP; Zinn, *SNCC*, 24.

25. Ibid.

26. Ibid.; "350 Negro Student Demonstrators Held in South Carolina Stockade," *New York Times*, March 16, 1960, 1; "Text of address by Herbert L. Wright," March 16, 1960, box E15, part 3, NAACP-LOC.

27. See Wittner, *Rebels Against War*, 171–72; Zinn, *SNCC*, 21–23.

28. Lewis, *Walking with the Wind*, 100.

29. Ibid., 101.

30. Ibid., 102.

31. Meier and Rudwick, *CORE*, 106–7.

32. White, "The Tallahassee Sit-Ins and CORE," 118.

33. "Who Leads the Sit-Downs? This Family Is Typical," *Southern Patriot*, April 1960, 1, 3; "Group 3," March 14, 1960, box 289, part 3, NAACP-LOC.

34. Patricia Stephens, quoted in "8 Negroes Choose Jail In 'Sacrifice,'" *New York Times*, March 19, 1960, 8. See also Meier and Rudwick, *CORE*, 107. King, quoted in "Sit-Ins Vow to go to Jail for Justice," *Afro-American*, February 27, 1960, 5. "Notes from Florida Jailhouse," *Southern Patriot*, May 1960, 3; "CORE Members Arrested," *CORE-lator*, April 1960, 1.

35. Letter from Patricia Stephens to James Robinson, March 20, 1960, reel 19, CORE. See Due, *Freedom in the Family*, 70–82.

36. Letter to C. Kenzie Steele, Carson et al., eds., *The Papers of Martin Luther King*, vol. 5, 391.

37. Letter to Margaret Leonard from A. J. Muste, March 10, 1961, reel 89.20, A. J. Muste papers. See also Barton, *The Fellowship of Reconciliation*, 253; Robinson, *Abraham Went Out*, 118–19.

38. Letter from Patricia Stephens to James Robinson, April 18, 1960, reel 19, CORE.

39. Greenberg, ed., *A Circle of Trust*, 34.

40. "Recommendations of the Findings and Recommendations Committee," April 1960, box 1, MLK. See also Carson, *SNCC*, 22–24.

41. Len Holt, quoted in "Jail, not Bail," *Southern Patriot*, May 1960, 4. See also Fairclough, *To Redeem the Soul*, 65; Sellers, *The River of No Return*, 33–34.

42. James Lawson, "Nonviolent Way," *Southern Patriot*, April 1960, 1; "Student Movement: New Phase," *Southern Patriot*, November 1960, 4.

43. Interview with Julian Bond, CRDP.

44. "CORE Memorandum: The Meaning of the Sit-Ins," n.d., reel 18, part 21, NAACP.

45. Ibid. Eager to maintain its position as the leading civil rights organization, the NAACP's National Office took every opportunity to stress its role in the sit-ins. See "Role of the NAACP in the Sit-Ins," n.d.

46. "Memo from Ruby Hurley," March 23, 1960, reel 22, part 21, NAACP.

47. "NAACP Plans Student Defense," *New York Times*, March 18, 1960, 2; "1,700 Students Arrested During 1960. Defending Youths Top NAACP Goal," *Afro-American*, January 10, 1961, 7. Letter from Roy Wilkins to Edward King, September 1, 1961, reel 18, part 21, NAACP.

48. "1,700 Students Arrested," 7.

49. "Memorandum from James Farmer to Roy Wilkins," June 10, 1960, reel 18, part 21, NAACP.

50. "Negro Criticizes NAACP Tactics," *New York Times*, April 17, 1960, 32; Fairclough, *To Redeem the Soul*, 63–64; Robinson, *Abraham Went Out*, 120–22.

51. "Now it is a nice thing to go to jail," 5.

52. "1,700 Students Arrested During 1960," 7.

Chapter 3. From Sit-Ins to Jail-Ins

1. Meier and Rudwick, *CORE*, 113; James R. Robinson, "Jail-Not Bail," *CORE-lator*, September 1960, 3.

2. Meier and Rudwick, *CORE*, 104, 113, 116–19.

3. "Memorandum on sit-down demonstrations in South Carolina," n.d.; "350 Negro Student Demonstrators Held in South Carolina Stockade," *New*

York Times, March 16, 1960, 1, 27; "Five More Sit-Ins Given Sentences," *New York Times*, April 15, 1960, 8; Gaither, *Jailed-In*; "Students Prefer Jail-Ins to Bail-Outs," *Southern Patriot*, February 1961, 5; "Jail-Ins," *CORE-lator*, March 1961, 1; Carson, *In Struggle*, 32–34.

4. Gaither, *Jailed-In*.

5. Ibid.

6. Carson, *In Struggle*, 32.

7. Gaither, *Jailed-In*.

8. Interview with Adelaide Taitt, CRDP. See also Zinn, *SNCC*, 39.

9. Interview with Adelaide Taitt; "Released, Jailed Students Praised," *Afro-American*, March 18, 1961, 7; Carson, *In Struggle*, 33.

10. Gloster B. Current to Roy Wilkins, "NAACP Position on Jail, no Bail," February 9, 1961, reel 22, part 21, NAACP.

11. Raines, *My Soul Is Rested*, 109. At CORE orientation sessions, participants pledged to accept imprisonment over bail. Special Freedom Ride edition of the *CORE-lator*, May 1961.

12. See Barnes, *Journey from Jim Crow*, 157–59.

13. "Alabama Mobs Make Mockery of Mother's Day," *Richmond Afro-American*, May 20, 1961, 7.

14. "300 Attack 21 Student Riders," *Richmond Afro-American*, May 27, 1961, 6.

15. Dittmer, *Local People*, 90. See also Branch, *Parting the Waters*, 456–59.

16. Leslie W. Dunbar, "Freedom Ride," *New South*, July-August 1961, 9.

17. Branch, *Parting the Waters*, 470–72.

18. Interview with Dave Dennis, Circle archives.

19. "List of Freedom Rider arrests," May 24–May 28, 1961, file 2–144, MSSC.

20. Ibid.; "Five Riders Post Bond, 22 Others Still in Jail," *Jackson Daily News*, May 28, 1961, 1.

21. "Report of Meeting," Freedom Ride Coordinating Committee, May 26, 1961, reel 3, part 2, SCLC.

22. Branch, *Parting the Waters*, 139.

23. "Memorandum to Officers of All Branches, Youth Councils and College Chapters, State Conferences from Roy Wilkins," May 25, 1961, reel 12, part 21, NAACP; Telegram to John Johnson from Thurgood Marshall, May 19, 1961, reel 12, part 21, NAACP; "Message clarifying the position of the NAACP regarding the 'Freedom Rides,'" June 14, 1961, reel 12, part 21, NAACP.

24. "Mississippi Governor Urges Prison Guards to be 'Careful' With Riders," *Afro-American*, June 24, 1961, 3.

25. "Boss of Prison Reinstated," *Jackson Daily News*, June 2, 1961, 1.

26. "U.S. Judge Curbs 'Ride' Promoters," *Jackson Daily News*, June 2, 1961, 1.

27. "Riders May Take a Ride," *Jackson Daily News*, June 4, 1961, 3. For more on Parchman Farm, see Lipman, "Mississippi's Prison Experience," 685–755; Oshinsky, *Parchman Farm*; Taylor, *Down on Parchman Farm*.

28. Raines, *My Soul Is Rested*, 126–27. See also "Riders Taken to Parchman," *Jackson Daily News*, June 15, 1961, 1; Frank Holloway, "Travel Notes from a Deep South Tourist," *New South*, July-August 1961, 3–8.

29. "Minutes of a meeting of the Board of Commissioners, Mississippi State Penitentiary," June 14, 1961, folder 10, Albert Gordon Freedom Rider Collection.

30. Interview with Dion T. Diamond, CRDP.

31. See, for example, James Farmer, "Jailed in Mississippi," *CORE-lator*, August 1961, 1.

32. Taylor, *Down on Parchman Farm*, 171.

33. Barnett actually visited the Riders in Parchman himself, see Raines, *My Soul Is Rested*, 128; "Jailed Freedom Riders Visited," *CORE-lator*, June 1961, 1.

34. Interview with Isaac Reynolds, CRDP.

35. Raines, *My Soul Is Rested*, 127. See also Hampton and Fayer, eds., *Voices of Freedom*, 95–96.

36. Raines, *My Soul Is Rested*, 127; Levy, ed., *Let Freedom Ring*, 81; interview with Dion T. Diamond.

37. This apparent reluctance to brutalize women was far from typical of the treatment accorded female civil rights workers. See Payne, *I've Got the Light of Freedom*, 270–71.

38. "Report of Meeting," Freedom Ride Coordinating Committee, May 26, 1961; letter from Wyatt T. Walker appealing for volunteers, June 1, 1961, reel 3, part 2, SCLC.

39. "Report of Meeting," May 26, 1961; letter from Wyatt T. Walker, June 1, 1961. "Persons arrested in Jackson, Mississippi, commonly known as 'Freedom Riders,' July 6, 1961"; "Persons arrested in Jackson, Mississippi, July 9, 1961"; "Persons arrested in Jackson, Mississippi, July 16, 1961"; "Persons arrested in Jackson, Mississippi, July 21, 1961"; "Persons arrested in Jackson, Mississippi, July 23, 1961"; "Persons arrested in Jackson, Mississippi, July 24, 1961"; "Persons arrested in Jackson, Mississippi, July 29, 1961"; "Persons arrested in Jackson, Mississippi, July 30, 1961." See also "List of arrested Freedom Riders, May 24–May 28, 1961." All are located in files 2–144, MSSC.

40. "Persons arrested in Jackson, Mississippi, July 6, 1961"; "Persons arrested in Jackson, Mississippi, July 9, 1961."

41. Arsenault, *Freedom Rides*, 335.

42. Raines, *My Soul Is Rested*, 127, 128; Dittmer, *Local People*, 98.

43. See Raines, *My Soul Is Rested*.

44. Meier and Rudwick, *CORE*, 140.

45. See letters from Miriam Feingold to her parents, July 2 and July 9, 1961, reel 1, Miriam Feingold papers.

46. Hampton and Fayer, eds., *Voices of Freedom*, 96.

47. "State Will Be Asked To Pay Rider Costs," *Jackson Daily News*, July 14, 1961, 1; "Davis Still to Ask Help on 'Rider' Burden," *Jackson Daily News*, July 15, 1961, 1; Kunstler with Isenberg, *My Life as a Radical Lawyer*, 102–4.

48. Interview with Edwin King.

49. "Minutes of the meeting of the Board of Commissioners, Mississippi State Penitentiary, November 14, 1961," folder 10, Albert Gordon Freedom Rider Collection; extract from "Report to Governor Barnett et al.," April 19, 1962, folder 10, Albert Gordon Freedom Rider collection.

50. "Minutes of the Freedom Ride Coordinating Committee," August 3, 1961, reel 3, part 2, SCLC. See also Farmer, *Lay Bare the Heart*, 211–12; Meier and Rudwick, *CORE*, 142–43; Raines, *My Soul Is Rested*, 129; letter from Carl Rachlin to Norman Dorsen, October 15, 1963, reel 10, CORE.

51. For more on the issue of federal protection of the Riders, see Belknap, *Federal Law and Southern Order*, 77–87.

52. Lewis, *Walking with the Wind*, 176.

53. Schlanger, "Beyond the Hero Judge," 2,017; Oshinsky, *Worse Than Slavery*, 238–41.

54. "Memorandum to CORE groups from Gordon R. Carey," February 10, 1962, box 1, MLK.

55. Ibid.

Chapter 4. The Middle of the Iceberg

1. Quoted in Zinn, *SNCC*, 76.

2. Carson, *In Struggle*, 39–42; Garrow, *Bearing the Cross*, 161–69.

3. Howard Zinn, "Albany, Georgia: Report," August 31–December 10, 1962, 3, reel 120, SRC.

4. Ibid., 31; Branch, *Parting the Waters*, 528–29.

5. Carson, *In Struggle*, 56–58; Zinn, *SNCC*, 123–26.

6. Forman, *The Making*, 247–49; Hampton and Fayer, eds., *Voices of Freedom*, 99–100.

7. Carson, *In Struggle*, 58–60; Forman, *The Making*, 251; Branch, *Parting the Waters*, 536.

8. Branch, *Parting the Waters*, 535–36.

9. Garrow, *Bearing the Cross*, 180.

10. Raines, *My Soul Is Rested*, 361–62.

11. Watters, *Down to Now*, 161.

12. Statement of Annie Sue Herring, n.d., reel 37, SNCC.

13. See Zinn, "Albany, Georgia: Report," 31; "Widow of Jail Beating Victim Sues Ga. Police," *New York Times*, May 27, 1961, 19.

14. "Extended report on the Albany Movement," n.d., reel 37, SNCC; statement of Brenda Boone, n.d.; statement of Eliza Coe, n.d.; statement of Olivia Crawford, n.d.; statement of Pearlie Mae Fields, n.d.; statement of Samuel Gilford, n.d.; statement of Elijah Harris, n.d.; statement of Annie Sue Herring, n.d.; statement of Bobby Holloway, n.d.; statement of Ray Jones, December 13, 1961; statement of Ralph Moses, n.d.; statement of Robert Price, n.d.; statement of Lewis Roberts, n.d.; all on reel 37, SNCC.

15. Letter from Joan Browning to Faye, December 11, 1961 (no. 1); letter from Joan Browning to Faye, December 11, 1961 (no. 2); letter from Lenore to Joan Browning, n.d.; letter from Joan Browning to Faye, December 18, 1961; Letter from Joan Browning to Faye, December 17, 1961; all are in the Joan Browning papers.

16. Although Browning had already associated with the civil rights movement, her stay in jail had the greatest emotional impact. Browning, "Shiloh Witness," 71.

17. Ibid., 69.

18. Letter from Joan Browning to Faye, December 12, 1961, Joan Browning papers; Browning, "Shiloh Witness," 70–71.

19. "SNCC news release," May 24, 1963, reel 10, SNCC; "Notes from consultation program of Inter-Organization Women's Committee," March 15, 1964, folder 2, box 8, series 19, NCNW.

20. Interview with Jane Rambeau, MZOH.

21. Interview with Geneva Collier, MZOH.

22. Ibid.; interview with Mary Jones, MZOH.

23. See, for example, Fairclough, *To Redeem*, 107–8.

24. Hampton and Fayer, eds., *Voices of Freedom*, 108. This discussion draws upon the work of Karran Sanger's *When The Spirit Says Sing!*

25. Hampton and Fayer, eds., *Voices of Freedom*, 119–20.

26. Reagon, "Songs of the Civil Rights Movement," 135.

27. Farmer, *Lay Bare*, 8. See also Sanger, *When the Spirit Says Sing!*, 88.

28. Quoted Sanger, *When the Spirit Says Sing!*, 89.

29. Branch, *Parting the Waters*, 535–38; Hampton and Fayer, eds., *Voices of Freedom*, 102–3.

30. Forman, *The Making*, 259.

31. Abernathy, *And the Walls*, 204–5; Branch, *Parting the Waters*, 543–50; Fairclough, *To Redeem*, 88; Garrow, *Bearing the Cross*, 180–81; Hampton and Fayer, eds., *Voices of Freedom*, 103–5; Lewis, *King*, 147–48.

32. See Forman, *The Making*, 255–56.

33. Interview with Jane Rambeau, MZOH.

34. Lewis, *King*, 150–54.

35. "Transcript of telephone conversation between Ruby Hurley, Vernon Jordan, and Gloster Current," December 18, 1961, reel 8, part 20, NAACP. "Extended report by Charles Sherrod," n.d., reel 37, SNCC. See also Fairclough, *To Redeem*, 89–90; "'Total Victory' Battlecry at Albany," *Afro-American*, December 30, 1961, 8.

36. Branch, *Parting the Waters*, 550–51.

37. *Voice of the Movement*, June 1962, 2; "SCLC Protests Jailing of Expectant Mother in Jackson, Mississippi," May 3, 1962, reel 3, part 3, SCLC; "Jailing of Expectant Mother Draws Protest," *Afro-American*, May 12, 1962, 1; "SNCC News Release," April 30, 1962, reel 14, SNCC.

38. Branch, *Pillar of Fire*, 56. See also Olson, *Freedom's Daughters*, 212; "SNCC report," February 4, 1965, reel 37, SNCC.

39. Payne, "Men Led, but Women Organized," 1–5; Olson, *Freedom's Daughters*.

40. Interview with Geneva Collier, MZOH.

41. Abernathy, *And the Walls*, 213–14; Garrow, *Bearing the Cross*, 202–6.

42. Abernathy, *And the Walls*, 214–16.

43. Branch, *Parting the Waters*, 605–6; Fairclough, *To Redeem*, 102; Hampton and Fayer, eds., *Voices of Freedom*, 111.

44. Branch, *Parting the Waters*, 609–13; Lewis, *King*, 161.

45. For more on this subject, see Marshall, "The Protest Movement and the Law," 785–803.

46. Forman, *The Making*, 257–58; Garrow, *Bearing the Cross*, 210.

47. Fairclough, *To Redeem*, 107–8.

48. Watters, *Down to Now*, 124.

49. King, untitled paper on the Albany Movement, n.d., box 1, MLK.

50. Carson, *In Struggle*, 61.

51. See *Voice of the Movement*, 13:1, n.d; Salter, *Jackson*, 63–67. "Appeal from North Jackson NAACP Youth Council," January 28, 1963, box E9, part 3, NAACP-LOC. Also see box E9, part 3, NAACP-LOC.

52. Moody, *Coming of Age*, 273–76; Salter, *Jackson*, 143–46.

53. "Jackson Police Jail 600 Negro Children," *New York Times*, June 1, 1963, 1, 8; Moody, *Coming of Age*, 279–80.

54. "Wilkins is Seized in Jackson, Mississippi," *New York Times*, June 2, 1963, 70. See Salter, *Jackson*, 154; Wilkins, *Standing Fast*, 132–36.

55. Letter to Roy Wilkins from Percy E. Sutton, June 3, 1963, Box A231, part 3, NAACP-LOC.

56. Branch, *Parting the Waters*, 816.

57. See Dittmer, *Local People*, 167–68; Ed King, untitled essay on the Jackson Movement, n.d., Edwin King papers (in author's possession); Salter, *Jackson*, 151–53; Ryan, "Leading from the Back," 43–50.

58. Interview with Edwin King by author.

59. "Militancy Grows in Jackson Drive," *New York Times*, June 17, 1963, 1; "Jackson Negroes Suspend Protest," *New York Times*, June 18, 1963, 23. See also Dittmer, *Local People*, 163–68; Salter, *Jackson*, 198–201, 207–11; "Summary Minutes of the 54th Annual Convention, supplement to part 1, Minutes of the Board of Directors," reel 5, NAACP.

60. For more on the positive role of interorganizational conflict between the NAACP and the nonviolent direct-action civil rights organizations, see Meier and Bracey, "The NAACP as a Reform Movement, 1909–1965," 3–10; Ling, "Uneasy Alliance," 43–58.

61. "Memorandum to Roy Wilkins from Robert Carter," September 16, 1963, box A43, part 3, NAACP-LOC; "Memorandum to Roy Wilkins from Robert Carter," November 27, 1963, box 1,189, part 5, NAACP-LOC; "Draft proposal for establishment of National Bail and Appeal Bond Committee," n.d., box 1,189, part 5, NAACP-LOC; "NAACP has put up $268,750 in bail for demonstrators," December 13, 1963, box A43, part 3, NAACP-LOC; "Memorandum to state presidents from Roy Wilkins," March 5, 1954, box A43, part 3, NAACP-LOC.

62. "Civil Disobedience and the Law," *New South*, October-November 1963, 24–28; Mary King, *Freedom Song*, 159–60.

63. "Fact Sheet. Americus, Georgia," n.d., reel 37, SNCC.

64. "Jailed on Death Penalty Charge," *CORE-lator*, September 1963, 1.

65. "Strict Law Enforcement Stifles Negroes' Drive in Americus, Ga.," *New York Times*, September 29, 1963, 80; "Fact Sheet. Americus, Georgia," n.d., reel 37, SNCC; "Desperately Needed: Prayers, Funds, Protest!" n.d., reel 22, CORE.

66. "Sworn deposition of Lena Turner," September 10, 1963, reel 37, SNCC; "sworn depositions of Lorena Barnum; Robertina Freeman; Eliza Thomas; Emma Jean Times taken on September 13, 1963," reel 37, SNCC; Danny Lyon, *Memories*, 80–81. See also Mary King, *Freedom Song*, 159–62.

67. Tuck, *Beyond Atlanta*, 176–80.

68. Letter from Zev Aelony to "Friends," September 14, 1963 (no. 1); letter from Zev Aelony to "Friends," September 14, 1963 (no. 2); letter from Zev Aelony to Marcia, September 28, 1963; all on reel 22, CORE; interview with Zev Aelony by author.

69. Letter from Gordon Carey to Zev Aelony, October 15, 1963, reel 22, CORE.

70. See James Farmer, *Lay Bare the Heart*, 243–45; "List of intimidation in Plaquemine, Louisiana," n.d., box 4, CORE-SRO.

71. "List of intimidation in Plaquemine, Louisiana," n.d., box 4, CORE-SRO; Farmer, *Lay Bare the Heart*, 246–52; "The Plaquemine Story," *CORE-lator*, September 1963, 1.

72. Quoted in Fairclough, *Race and Democracy*, 329–30.

73. "Perez Readies 'Dungeon' for Civil Rights 'Demonstrators,'" November 2, 1963, box 6, CORE-SRO; statement by Betty Binder on visit to Fort St. Philip, n.d., box 6, CORE-SRO.

Chapter 5. This Lousy Hole

1. See Marsh, *God's Long Summer*, 49–81. For more on the murder of Schwerner, Goodman, and Chaney, see Huie, *Three Lives for Mississippi*; Belfrage, *Freedom Summer*; Mills, *Like A Holy Crusade*; Cagin and Dray, *We Are Not Afraid*.

2. Belfrage, *Freedom Summer*, 17, 23.

3. Ibid., 132.

4. Ibid., 115.

5. McAdam, *Freedom Summer*, 101.

6. Letter to June and Bonny from Peter Milenburg, June 1965, Edwin King papers.

7. Belfrage, *Freedom Summer*, 118.

8. Letter to John and Bonny from Peter Milenburg, June 1965; letter to unidentified recipient from Peter Milenburg, June 9, 1965, both in Edwin King papers.

9. Estes, *I Am a Man!*, 75.

10. Hill, *Deacons for Defense*, 203.

11. Payne, "Men Led, but Women Organized," 1–6.

12. See Estes, *I Am a Man!*; Hill, *Deacons for Defense*; Tyson, *Radio Free Dixie*.

13. Estes, *I Am a Man!*, 75.

14. Mary King, *Freedom Song*, 177.

15. "SNCC news release," February 20, 1964, reel 14, SNCC. The Inter-Organization Women's Committee also issued a report of a white woman being beaten by prisoners. See "Notes From Consultation Program of Inter-Organization Women's Committee," March 15, 1964, folder 2, box 8, series 19, NCNW.

16. Interview with Fannie Lou Hamer, CRDP; Marsh, *God's Long Summer*, 18–21; Mills, *This Little Light of Mine*, 59–60.

17. Tyson, *Radio Free Dixie*, 1–2.

18. Marsh, *God's Long Summer*, 20–21.

19. See also "'They Tried to Destroy Our Self-Respect' HU Coed Tells of Weeks as Jailed Rider," *Afro-American*, August 19, 1961, 8; Belfrage, *Freedom Summer*, 142–43.

20. Transcript of Dorothy Height, interviewed by William B. Williams, broadcast by WNEW Radio, June 6, 1963, reel 22, CORE; "Sex Abuses in Jackson Jail Told," *Afro-American*, June 15, 1963, 1.

21. "NCNW News Release," June 10, 1963, folder 2, box 8, series 19, NCNW.

22. Details of the meeting can be found in "Consultation Program: Inter-Organization Women's Committee," March 14–16, 1964, folder 2, box 8, series 19, NCNW. For reports of the abuse of the two white women working in Albany, see "SNCC news release," May 24, 1963, reel 10, SNCC; extracts of "Georgia Civil Rights Worker: Why Does She Do It?—'I Want To Be Free,'" *Washington Post*, August 31, 1963, reprinted in "Two Courageous Women Witness for Equal Justice," *Congressional Record*, September 4, 1963, folder 14, box 5, series 10, NCNW.

23. "Consultation Program: Inter-Organization Women's Committee," March 14–16, 1964.

24. A couple of exceptions to this silence are McGuire, "It Was Like All of Us Had Been Raped," 906–31; McGuire, *At the Dark End of the Street*.

25. Belfrage, *Freedom Summer*, 118, 122–25.

26. Mary King, *Freedom Song*, 179–80.

27. Dion Diamond jail letter, number 5, March 14, 1964, Diamond papers.

28. Dion Diamond jail letter, number 4, March 1964, Diamond papers.

29. Dion Diamond jail letter, number 10, March 18, 1964, Diamond papers.

30. Ibid.; Dion Diamond jail letter, number 11, March 19, 1964, Diamond papers.

31. The entire poem is reproduced in Watters, *Down to Now*, 117–23. Watters does not identify the black minister who composed it.

32. Ibid.

33. Mills, *Like a Holy Crusade*, 165–79.

34. Garrow, *Bearing the Cross*, 292.

35. "Handbook for Freedom Army Recruits," 1964, box 22, MLK.

36. "Press Release, Selma, Alabama," February 1, 1965, reel 37, SNCC.

37. For more on the SCLC's use of nonviolence in Selma, see Garrow, *Protest at Selma*, 223–31.

Chapter 6. You Can't Jail the Revolution

1. Dittmer, *Local People*, 396.

2. Carson, *In Struggle*, 229–43; Meier and Rudwick, *CORE*, 415–25.

3. Fairclough, *Race and Democracy*, 382–95; Chafe, *Civilities and Civil Rights*, 243–51; Kirk, *Redefining the Color Line*, 162–66.

4. Fairclough, *Race and Democracy*, 417–23.

5. For examples of studies that emphasize the impact of police brutality, see Grady-Willis, *Challenging U.S. Apartheid*; Countryman, *Up South*.

6. Hill, *Deacons for Defense*; Fairclough, *Race and Democracy*, 382–83.

7. Cecelski, *Along Freedom Road*, 105–15.

8. For more on COINTELPRO, see Blackstock, *COINTELPRO*; Churchill and Wall, *The COINTELPRO Papers*; Churchill and Wall, *Agents of Repression*; O'Reilly, *Racial Matters*.

9. This account is taken from literature produced by members of the African American community in Birmingham, Alabama. See "Bryant-Williams," folder 1.8, Birmingham Police Department Files. For another account, see Orange, *From Segregation to Civil Rights*. For a community-level study of the ABLF, see Widell, "The Power Belongs To Us," 136–80.

10. Schutz, "Going to Hell," PhD Diss., 98.

11. "The Repression of the RNA," *Black Scholar*, October 1971.

12. A fourth man, Clarence Harrison, was also indicted for the barn burning, but he immediately isolated himself from the other three by pleading guilty.

13. This discussion draws upon the work in Schutz, "Going to Hell," PhD Diss.

14. See, for example, "Jails are the First Black Concentration Camps," *Black Panther*, May 18, 1968, 4, 26; "Charles Bursey: Another Political Prisoner," *Black Panther*, August 16, 1968, 10.

15. "New York's Tombs of Torture," *Black Panther*, August 30, 1969, 8. See also, for example, "Prisoner's Report From Alameda County Jail," *Black Panther*, June 10, 1968, 16; "Conditions of Jails—From Members of the Panther N.Y. 21," *Black Panther*, July 5, 1969, 9. The paper also regularly carried letters from imprisoned party members.

16. Grant, "Our Mecklenburg County Jail from the Inside," and Parker, "Statement of Conditions at Other Camps and Prisons in North Carolina," both in NCPPC newsletter, 1, no. 7, Reddy papers.

17. See, for example, Glick, *Prisons, Protest, and Politics*; Browning, *Prison Life*; Berkman, *Opening the Gates*; Irwin, *Prisons in Turmoil*; Wright, *The Politics of Punishment*.

18. Davis, *If They Come in the Morning,* 37; "Charles Bursey: Another Political Prisoner," *Black Panther*, August 16, 1968, 10.

19. Davis, *If They Come in the Morning,* 50–57.

20. "Appeal for help with convictions of Ron Williams and Weyland Bryant," July 1, 1971, folder 1.8, Birmingham Police Department Files; NCPPC newsletter, vol. 1, no. 3, 4, folder 13, box 1, Reddy papers.

21. Given that a high proportion of black crime was committed within their own communities, acceptance of this concept was far from universal among African Americans.

22. Cummins, *The Rise and Fall,* 143.

23. In less than a year, police harassment and brutality had destroyed the New Orleans chapter. See Fairclough, *Race and Democracy,* 424–27.

24. "New Orleans Prisoners Rise Up—Demand Resignation of D.A. Jim Garrison," *Black Panther*, August 2, 1971, 3, 11.

25. Herman Wallace, "The Rise and Fall of the Angola Prison Chapter of the Black Panther Party," n.d., http://www.itsabouttimebpp.com/Political_ Prisoners/pdf/The_Rise_and_Fall_of_the_Angola_Prison_Chapter_of_the_ Black_Panther_Party.pdf, accessed April 16, 2012.

26. Quoted in Schlanger, "Beyond the Hero Judge," 2,017.

27. Ibid.; Greenberg, *Crusades in the Courts,* 440–77; Feeley and Rubin, *Judicial Policy Making.*

28. For more on the Joan Little case, see "Testimony of Joan Little, August 11–13, 1975," folder 1, box 1, James Reston Papers; Reston, *The Innocence of Joan Little*; McNeil, "The Body, Sexuality, and Self-Defense," 235–61; McGuire, *At the Dark End,* ch. 8.

29. Letter from Southern Poverty Law Center on Joan Little case, box 119, part 5, NAACP-LOC; Reston, *The Innocence of Joan Little,* 145.

30. Reston, *The Innocence of Joan Little,* 48.

31. Schutz, "Going to Hell," 304–8.

32. See, for example, Jeffries, *Comrades*; Joseph, *The Black Power Movement*; Ogbar, *Black Power*; Franklin, "Introduction: New Black Power Studies," 463–66; Joseph, "Black Liberation Without Apology, 2–17."

Conclusion

1. Foucault, *Discipline and Punish.*

2. For more on the positive impact of conflict between the NAACP and SNCC, CORE, and the SCLC, see Meier and Bracey, "The NAACP as a Reform Movement," 3–30.

3. "Some Question Why Rosa Parks Should Be Pardoned By Alabama," *Montgomery Advertiser*, July 26, 2006.

4. "Family seeking Kennard Pardon," *Clarion-Ledger*, April 13, 2006, B1; "Pardoning Kennard Still Sought," *Clarion-Ledger*, May 15, 2006, B1; "Pardon Unlikely for Civil Rights Advocate," *New York Times*, May 4, 2006. My thanks to Professor John Howard for bringing this to my attention.

5. "Witness: Man Innocent in '60 Burglary," *Hattiesburg American*, January 1, 2006, A9. While Governor Barbour insisted he could not pardon Kennard, those seeking to exonerate the Mississippian succeeded in securing a pardon by Judge Helfrich of the Circuit Court of Forrest County in May 2006. The Mississippi State Supreme Court upheld the ruling in August 2007. See Jerry Mitchell, "Forrest County Judge Exonerates Late Korean War Veteran Clyde Kennard," *Clarion-Ledger*, May 17, 2006.

Bibliography

Archival Sources

Adickes, Sandra. Papers. State Historical Society of Wisconsin, Madison.

Association of Southern Women for the Prevention of Lynching Papers. Microfilm. Alderman Library, University of Virginia, Charlottesville.

Behind the Veil Oral History Collections. David Rubenstein Library, Duke University, North Carolina.

Bernard, Jacqueline. Papers. State Historical Society of Wisconsin, Madison.

Birmingham Police Department Files. Birmingham Public Library, Birmingham, Alabama.

Black Panther Documents. Microfilm. Harlan Hatcher Graduate Library, University of Michigan, Ann Arbor.

Browning, Joan. Papers. Robert W. Woodruff Library, Emory University, Atlanta, Georgia.

Circle Archives Oral History Collection. Southern Regional Council Offices, Atlanta, Georgia.

Civil Rights Congress Papers. Microfilm. Manuscript Division, Library of Congress, Washington, D.C.

Civil Rights Documentation Oral History Project. Howard University, Washington, D.C. (CRDP).

Civil Rights Scrapbook. Birmingham Public Library, Birmingham, Alabama.

Commission for Interracial Cooperation Papers. Microfilm. Manuscript Division, Library of Congress, Washington, D.C.

Congress of Racial Equality Papers, 1941–1967. Microfilm. Alderman Library, University Of Virginia, Charlottesville (CORE).

Congress of Racial Equality Southern Regional Office Papers. State Historical Society of Wisconsin, Madison (CORE-SRO).

Connor, Theophilus Eugene "Bull." Papers. Birmingham Public Library, Birmingham, Alabama.

Diamond, Dion T. Notebook. State Historical Society of Wisconsin, Madison.

FBI File on the Black Panther Party in North Carolina. Microfilm. Harlan Hatcher Graduate Library, University of Michigan, Ann Arbor.

Feingold, Miriam. Papers. State Historical Society of Wisconsin, Madison.

Fellowship of Reconciliation Papers. Swarthmore College Peace Collection, McCabe Library, Swarthmore, Pennsylvania (FOR).

Gordon, Albert. Freedom Rider Collection. McCain Library and Archives, University of Southern Mississippi, Hattiesburg.

Gordon, Linda. Papers. State Historical Society of Wisconsin, Madison.

Hambee, Lillian. Papers. Mount Zion Civil Rights Museum, Albany, Georgia.

Hamer, Fannie Lou. Papers. Manuscript Division, Library of Congress, Washington, D.C.

Hampton, Benjamin. Papers. Mount Zion Civil Rights Museum, Albany, Georgia.

Harris, Anthony J. Civil Rights Memoir. McCain Library, University of Southern Mississippi, Hattiesburg.

King, Edwin. Papers. Coleman Library, Tougaloo College, Jackson, Mississippi.

King, Martin Luther, Jr. Papers. Martin Luther King Jr. Center for Nonviolent Social Change, Atlanta, Georgia (MLK).

King, Slater. Papers. Mount Zion Civil Rights Museum, Albany, Georgia.

Mississippi State Sovereignty Commission Records. State Historical Society of Mississippi, Jackson, Mississippi (MSSC).

Mount Zion Civil Rights Oral History Project. Mount Zion Civil Rights Museum, Albany, Georgia (MZOH).

National Association for the Advancement of Colored People Papers. Microfilm. Alderman Library, University of Virginia, Charlottesville (NAACP).

National Association for the Advancement of Colored People Papers. Manuscript Division, Library of Congress, Washington, D.C. (NAACP-LOC).

National Council of Negro Women Papers. Mary McCleod Bethune House, Washington, D.C. (NCNW).

Raper, Arthur. Papers. Special Collections, University of North Carolina, Chapel Hill.

Reddy, Thomas. Papers. Special Collections, University of North Carolina, Charlotte.

Reston, James. Papers. Special Collections, University of North Carolina, Chapel Hill.

Rustin, Bayard. Papers. Microfilm. Main Library, University of Sheffield, UK.

Social Action Vertical File. State Historical Society of Wisconsin, Madison.

Southern Christian Leadership Conference Papers. Microfilm. Alderman Library, University of Virginia, Charlottesville (SCLC).

Southern Regional Council Papers. Microfilm. Alderman Library, University of Virginia, Charlottesville (SRC).

Student Nonviolent Coordinating Committee Papers. Microfilm. Alderman Library, University of Virginia, Charlottesville (SNCC).

Published Sources

Abbott, Jack Henry. *In the Belly of the Beast: Letters from Prison.* New York: Vintage Books, 1981.

Abernathy, Ralph. *And the Walls Came Tumbling Down: An Autobiography.* New York: Harper and Row, 1989.

Allen, James, ed. *Without Sanctuary: Lynching Photography in America.* Santa Fe, New Mexico: Twin Palms, 2000.

Ansbro, John J. *Martin Luther King, Jr.: The Making of a Mind.* New York: Orbis, 1983.

Arsenault, Raymond. *Freedom Riders: 1961 and the Struggle for Racial Justice.* Oxford: Oxford University Press, 2006.

Atkins, Burton M., and Henry R. Glick, eds. *Prisons, Protest, and Politics.* Englewood Cliffs, New Jersey: Prentice-Hall, 1972.

Ayers, Edward L. *Vengeance and Justice: Crime and Punishment in the Nineteenth-Century South.* Oxford: Oxford University Press, 1984.

———. *The Promise of the New South: Life after Reconstruction.* New York: Oxford University Press, 1992.

Badillo, Herman, and Milton Haynes. *A Bill of No Rights: Attica and the American Prison System.* New York: Outerbridge and Lazard, 1972.

Baldwin, Lewis V. *There Is a Balm in Gilead: The Cultural Roots of Martin Luther King, Jr.* Minneapolis: Fortress, 1991.

Banks, Mary. "Trailblazers: Women in the Montgomery Bus Boycott." In *Women in the Civil Rights Movement: Trailblazers and Torchbearers, 1941–1965*, edited by Vicki Crawford, Jacqueline Anne Rouse, and Barbara Woods, 71–84. New York: Carlson, 1990.

Barkan, Steven E. *Protesters on Trial: Criminal Justice in the Southern Civil Rights and Vietnam Antiwar Movements*. New Brunswick, New Jersey: Rutgers University Press, 1985.

Barnes, Catherine. *Journey from Jim Crow: The Desegregation of Southern Transport*. New York: Columbia University Press, 1983.

Bartley, Numan. *The New South, 1945–1980: The Story of the South's Modernization*. Baton Rouge: Louisiana State University Press, 1995.

Barton, Betty Lynn. "The Fellowship of Reconciliation: Pacifism, Labor, and Social Welfare, 1915–1960." Ph.D. dissertation, Florida State University, 1974.

Belfrage, Sally. *Freedom Summer*. London: Mayflower, 1965.

Belknap, Michael J. *Federal Law and Southern Order: Racial Violence and Constitutional Conflict in the Post-Brown South*. Athens: University of Georgia Press, 1987.

Bennett, Lerone, Jr. *What Manner of Man: A Biography of Martin Luther King, Jr.* Chicago: Johnson, 1968.

Berkman, Ronald. *Opening the Gates: The Rise of the Prisoners' Movement*. Lexington, Mass.: Gower Press, 1980.

Berry, Mary F. *Black Resistance, White Law: A History of Constitutional Racism in America*. New York: Penguin, 1994.

———. "Judging Morality: Sexual Behavior and Legal Consequences in the Late Nineteenth-Century South." *Journal of American History* 78 (December 1991): 834–56.

Blackstock, Nelson. *COINTELPRO: The FBI's Secret War on Political Freedom*. New York: Pathfinder, 1988.

Branch, Taylor. *Parting the Waters: Martin Luther King and the Civil Rights Movement, 1954–63*. London: MacMillan, 1988.

———. *Pillar of Fire: America in the King Years, 1963–65*. New York: Simon and Schuster, 1998.

Bridges, George S., and Martha A. Myers. *Inequality, Crime and Social Control*. Boulder, Colo.: Westview Press, 1994.

Brinkley, Douglas. *Rosa Parks*. New York: Viking, 2000.

Brown, C. *Stagolee Shot Billy*. Cambridge: Harvard University Press, 2003.

Brown, Judith M. *Gandhi and Civil Disobedience: The Mahatma in Indian Politics, 1928–1934*. Cambridge: Cambridge University Press, 1977.

Browning, Frank, and the editors of Ramparts magazine, eds. *Prison Life: A Study of the Explosive Conditions in America's Prisons*. New York: Harper and Row, 1972.

Browning, Joan. "Shiloh Witness." In *Deep in Our Hearts: Nine White Women in the Freedom Movement*, by Constance Curry, Joan C. Browning, Dorothy Dawson Burlage, Penny Patch, Theresa Del Pozzo, Sue Thrasher, Elaine De-Lott Baker, Emmie Schrader Adams, and Casey Hayden, 37–84. Athens: University of Georgia Press, 2001.

Brundage, W. Fitzhugh. *Lynching in the New South: Georgia and Virginia, 1880–1930*. Chicago: University of Illinois Press, 1993.

———, ed. *Under Sentence of Death: Lynching in the South*. Chapel Hill: University of North Carolina Press, 1997.

Cagin, Seth, and Philip Dray. *We Are Not Afraid: The Story of Goodman, Schwerner, and Chaney, and the Civil Rights Campaign for Mississippi*. New York: Macmillan, 1998.

Cameron, James. *A Time of Terror: A Survivor's Story*. Baltimore: Black Classic Press, 1982.

Capeci, Dominic J. "The Lynching of Cleo Wright: Federal Protection of Constitutional Rights During World War II." *Journal of American History* 72 (March 1986): 859–87.

Carleton, Mark Thomas. *Politics and Punishment: The History of the Louisiana State Penal System*. Baton Rouge: Louisiana State University Press, 1971.

Carmichael, Stokeley, and Charles V. Hamilton. *Black Power: The Politics of Liberation in America*. New York: Random House, 1967.

Carroll, Leo. *Hacks, Blacks, and Cons: Race Relations in a Maximum Security Prison*. Lexington, Mass.: Lexington Books, 1974.

Carson, Clayborne. *In Struggle: SNCC and the Black Awakening of the 1960s*. Cambridge: Harvard University Press, 1981.

———, ed. *The Eyes on the Prize Civil Rights Reader: Documents, Speeches, and Firsthand Accounts from the Black Freedom Struggle, 1954–1990*. New York: Viking, 1991.

———, ed. *The Papers of Martin Luther King, Jr., vol. 3: Birth of a New Age, December 1955–December 1956*. Berkeley: University of California Press, 1997.

———, ed. *The Papers of Martin Luther King, Jr., vol. 5: Threshold of a New Decade, January 1959–December 1960*. Berkeley: University of California Press, 2005.

Cecelski, David. *Along Freedom Road: Hyde County, North Carolina, and the*

Fate of Black Schools in the South. Chapel Hill: University of North Carolina Press, 1994.

Chadbourn, James H. *Lynching and the Law*. Chapel Hill: University of North Carolina Press, 1933.

Chafe, William. *Civilities and Civil Rights: Greensboro, North Carolina, and the Black Struggle for Freedom*. Oxford: Oxford University Press, 1980.

———. *Remembering Jim Crow: African Americans Tell about Life in the Segregated South*. New York: The New Press, 2001.

Cha-Jua, Sundiata, and Clarence Lang. "The 'Long Movement' as Vampire: Temporal and Spatial Fallacies in Recent Black Freedom Studies." *Journal of African American History* 92 (Winter 2007): 265–88.

Chappell, Marissa, Jenny Hutchinson, and Brian Ward. "'Dress modestly, neatly . . . as if you were going to church': Respectability, Class, and Gender in the Montgomery Bus Boycott and the Early Civil Rights Movement." In *Gender in the Civil Rights Movement*, edited by Peter Ling and Sharon Monteith, 69–100. New Brunswick: Rutgers, 2004.

Chevigny, Paul. *Cops and Rebels: A Study of Provocation*. New York: Pantheon Books, 1972.

Churchill, Ward, and Jim Vander Wall. *The COINTELPRO Papers: Documents from the FBI's Secret Wars against Dissent in the United States*. Boston: South End Press, 1990.

———. *Agents of Repression: The FBI's Secret Wars against the Black Panther Party and the American Indian Movement*. Boston: South End Press, 1990.

"Civil Liberties Docket," 5, no. 3 (June 1960). <http://sunsite.berkeley.edu/meiklejohn/meik-5_3/>. Accessed July 31, 2005.

Cleaver, Kathleen, and George Katsiaficas, eds. *Liberation, Imagination, and the Black Panther Party: A New Look at the Panthers and Their Legacy*. New York: Routledge, 2001.

Cluster, Dick, ed. *They Should Have Served that Cup of Coffee: 7 Radicals Remember the '60s*. Boston: South End Press, 1979.

Colaiaco, James A. *Martin Luther King, Jr.: Apostle of Militant Nonviolence*. London: Macmillan, 1988.

Colburn, David R. *Racial Change and Community Crisis: St. Augustine, Florida, 1877–1980*. New York: Columbia University Press, 1985.

Cole, David. *No Equal Justice: Race and Class in the American Criminal Justice System*. New York: New Press, 1999.

Countryman, Matthew. *Up South: Civil Rights and Black Power in Philadelphia*. Philadelphia: University of Pennsylvania Press, 2006.

Crawford, Vicki, Jacqueline Rouse, and Barbara Woods, eds. *Women in the Civil*

Rights Movement: Trailblazers and Torchbearers, 1941–1965. Brooklyn: Carlson, 1990.

Cummins, Eric. *The Rise and Fall of California's Radical Prison Movement*. Stanford: Stanford University Press, 1994.

Curry, Constance, Joan C. Browning, Dorothy Dawson Burlage, Penny Patch, Theresa Del Pozzo, Sue Thrasher, Elaine DeLott Baker, Emmie Schrader Adams, and Casey Hayden. *Deep in Our Hearts: Nine White Women in the Freedom Movement*. Athens: University of Georgia Press, 2001.

Curtin, Mary Ellen. "Legacies of Struggle: Black Prisoners in the Making of Postbellum Alabama, 1865–1895." Ph.D. dissertation, Duke University, 1992.

———. *Black Prisoners and Their World, Alabama, 1865–1900*. Charlottesville: University Press of Virginia, 2000.

Davis, Allison, Burleigh Bradford Gardner, and Mary R. Gardner. *Deep South: A Social Anthropological Study of Caste and Class*. Chicago: University of Chicago Press, 1941.

Davis, Angela. *If They Come in the Morning: Voices of Resistance*. London: Orbach and Chambers, 1971.

de la Roche, Roberta Senechal. "The Sociogenesis of Lynching." In *Under Sentence of Death: Lynching in the South*, edited by W. Fitzhugh Brundage, 48–76. Chapel Hill: University of North Carolina Press, 1997.

Dittmer, John. *Local People: The Struggle for Civil Rights in Mississippi*. Urbana: University of Illinois Press, 1994.

Du Bois, W.E.B. *The Souls of Black Folk*. In *Three Negro Classics*, 207–390. New York: Avon, 1965.

Due, Tananarive, and Patricia Stephens Due. *Freedom in the Family: A Mother-Daughter Memoir of the Fight for Civil Rights*. New York: One World, 2003.

Dulaney, W. Marvin. *Black Police in America*. Bloomington: Indiana University Press, 1996.

Dyson, Michael Eric. *I May Not Get There with You: The True Martin Luther King, Jr*. New York: Free Press, 2000.

Eagles, Charles. "Toward New Histories of the Civil Rights Era." *Journal of Southern History* 66 (November 2000): 815–48.

Erenrich, Susie, ed. *Freedom Is a Constant Struggle: An Anthology of the Mississippi Civil Rights Movement*. Montgomery, Ala.: Black Belt Press, 1999.

Eskew, Glenn T. *But for Birmingham: The Local and National Movements in the Civil Rights Struggle*. Chapel Hill: University of North Carolina Press, 1997.

Estes, Steve. *I Am a Man!: Race, Manhood, and the Civil Rights Movement*. Chapel Hill: University of North Carolina Press, 2006.

Evers, Myrlie B. *For Us, the Living*. Jackson: University Press of Mississippi, 1996.

Fairclough, Adam. "The Preachers and the People: The Origins and Early Years of the Southern Christian Leadership Conference, 1955–1959." *Journal of Southern History* 52 (August 1986): 403–40.

———. *To Redeem the Soul of America: The Southern Leadership Conference and Martin Luther King, Jr.* Athens: University of Georgia Press, 1987.

———. *Martin Luther King, Jr.* Athens: University of Georgia Press, 1990.

———. *Race and Democracy: The Civil Rights Struggle in Louisiana, 1915–1972.* Athens: University of Georgia Press, 1995.

Farmer, James. *Lay Bare the Heart: An Autobiography of the Civil Rights Movement*. New York: Arbor House, 1985.

Feeley, Malcolm, and Edward Rubin. *Judicial Policy Making and the Modern State: How the Courts Reformed America's Prisons*. Cambridge: Cambridge University Press, 1998.

Finnegan, Terence Robert. "'At the Hands of Parties Unknown': Lynching in Mississippi and South Carolina, 1881–1940." Ph.D. dissertation, University of Illinois at Urbana-Champaign, 1993.

Fischer, Louis, ed. *The Essential Gandhi: An Anthology*. London: George Allen, 1962.

Foner, Eric, ed. *The Black Panthers Speak*. New York: Da Capo Press, 1995.

Forman, James. *The Making of Black Revolutionaries*. Washington, D.C.: Open Hand, 1985.

Foucault, Michael. *Discipline and Punish: The Birth of the Prison*. Trans. Alan Sheridan. London: Penguin, 1977.

Franklin, H. Bruce. *The Victim as Criminal and Artist: Literature from the American Prison*. New York: Oxford University Press, 1978.

Franklin, V. P. "New Black Power Studies: National, International, and Transnational Perspectives." *Journal of African American History* 92 (Fall 2007): 463–66.

Friedman, Lawrence M. *Crime and Punishment in American History*. New York: Harper Collins, 1993.

Gaither, Thomas. *Jailed-In*. New York: League for Industrial Democracy, 1961.

Gandhi, Mohandas K. *An Autobiography or The Story of My Experiments with Truth*. Harmondsworth: Penguin, 1982 (1927).

Garrow, David. *Protest at Selma: Martin Luther King, Jr. and the Voting Rights Act of 1965*. New Haven: Yale University Press, 1978.

———. *Bearing the Cross: Martin Luther King, Jr., and the Southern Christian Leadership Conference*. New York: William, Morrow and Company, 1986.

———. *The Walking City: The Montgomery Bus Boycott, 1955–1956.* Brooklyn: Carlson, 1989.

———, ed. *Atlanta, Georgia, 1960–1961: Sit-Ins and Student Activism.* Brooklyn: Carlson, 1989.

———, ed. *We Shall Overcome: The Civil Rights Movement in the United States in the 1950s and 1960s, vol. 2.* Brooklyn: Carlson, 1989.

Grady-Willis, Winston A. "The Black Panther Party: State Repression and Political Prisoners." In *The Black Panther Party (Reconsidered)*, edited by Charles E. Jones, 417–36. Baltimore: Black Classic Press, 1998.

———. *Challenging U.S. Apartheid: Atlanta and Black Struggles for Human Rights, 1960–1977.* Durham: Duke University Press, 2006.

Graetz, Robert. *A White Preacher's Memoir: The Montgomery Bus Boycott.* Montgomery, Ala.: Black Belt Press, 1998.

Greenberg, Cheryl Lynn, ed. *A Circle of Trust: Remembering SNCC.* New Brunswick, New Jersey: Rutgers University Press, 1998.

Greenberg, Jack. *Crusaders in the Courts: How a Dedicated Band of Lawyers Fought for the Civil Rights Revolution.* New York: HarperCollins, 1994.

Gregg, Richard B. *The Power of Non-Violence.* London: George Routledge, 1936.

Grier, William, and Price Cobbs. *Black Rage.* New York: Basic Books, 1996.

Griffin, Larry J., Paula Clark, and Joanne C. Sandberg. "Narrative and Event: Lynching and Historical Sociology." In *Under Sentence of Death: Lynching in the South*, edited by W. Fitzhugh Brundage, 24–47. Chapel Hill: University of North Carolina Press, 1997.

Hall, Jacquelyn Dowd. *Revolt Against Chivalry: Jessie Daniel Ames and the Women's Campaign Against Lynching.* New York: Columbia University Press, 1979.

———. "The Long Civil Rights Movement and the Political Uses of the Past." *Journal of American History* 91 (March 2005): 1,233–63.

Hamlet, Janice D. "Fannie Lou Hamer: The Unquenchable Spirit of the Civil Rights Movement." *Journal of Black Studies* 26 (May 1996): 560–76.

Hampton, Henry, and Steve Fayer, eds. *Voices of Freedom: An Oral History of the Civil Rights Movement from the 1950s through the 1980s.* New York: Bantam Books, 1990.

Heath, G. Louis, ed. *The Black Panther Leaders Speak: Huey P. Newton, Bobby Seale, Eldridge Cleaver and Company Speak Out Through the Black Panther Party Official Newspaper.* Metuchen, New Jersey: Scarecrow, 1976.

———, ed. *Off the Pigs!: The History and Literature of the Black Panther Party.* Metuchen, New Jersey: Scarecrow, 1976.

Henderson, Errol A. "The Lumpenproletariat as Vanguard?: The Black Panther

Party, Social Transformation, and Pearson's Analysis of Huey Newton." *Journal of Black Studies* 28 (November 1997): 171–99.

Henderson, Thelton. "The Law and Civil Rights: The Justice Department in the South." *New University Thought* 3 (1963): 36–45.

Henry, Aaron, and Constance Curry. *Aaron Henry: The Fire Ever Burning*. Jackson: University Press of Mississippi, 2000.

Herndon, Angelo. *Let Me Live*. New York: Random House, 1937.

Hill, Lance. *The Deacons for Defense: Armed Resistance and the Civil Rights Movement*. Chapel Hill: University of North Carolina Press, 2004.

Hilliard, David, and Lewis Cole. *This Side of Glory: The Autobiography of David Hilliard and the Story of the Black Panther Party*. Boston: Little, Brown and Company, 1993.

Holland, Endesha Ida Mae. *From the Mississippi Delta: A Memoir*. Chicago: Lawrence Hill, 1997.

Howard, Walter T. "Vigilante Justice: Extra-Legal Executions in Florida, 1930–1940." Ph.D. dissertation, Florida State University, 1987.

Huie, William Bradford. *Three Lives for Mississippi*. London: Heinemann, 1965.

Irwin, John. *Prisons in Turmoil*. Boston: Little, Brown, 1980.

Jackson, Bruce. *Wake Up Dead Man: Hard Labor and Southern Blues*. Athens: University of Georgia Press, 1999.

Jackson, George. *Soledad Brother: The Prison Letters of George Jackson*. Harmondsworth, Middlesex: Penguin Books, 1970.

Jeffries, Judson L., ed. *Black Power in the Belly of the Beast*. Urbana: University of Illinois Press, 2006.

———, ed. *Comrades: A Local History of The Black Panther Party*. Bloomington: Indiana University Press, 2007.

Johnson, Roberta Ann. "The Prison Birth of Black Power." *Journal of Black Studies* 5 (June 1975): 395–414.

Jones, Charles, ed. *The Black Panther Party (Reconsidered)*. Baltimore: Black Classic Press, 1998.

Jospeh, Peniel E. "Black Liberation Without Apology: Reconceptualizing the Black Power Movement." *The Black Scholar* 31 (Fall/Winter 2001): 2–17.

———. *Waiting 'Til the Midnight Hour: A Narrative History of Black Power in America*. New York: Henry Holt, 2006.

———. "The Black Power Movement: A State of the Art." *Journal of American History* (December 2009): 1–36.

———, ed. *The Black Power Movement: Rethinking the Civil Rights-Black Power Era*. New York: Routledge, 2006.

Kapur, Sudarshan. *Raising up a Prophet: The African American Encounter with Gandhi*. Boston: Beacon Press, 1992.

Katz, Neil. "Radical Pacifism and the Contemporary American Peace Movement: The Committee for Nonviolent Action, 1957–1967." Ph.D. dissertation, University of Maryland, 1974.

Kelley, Robin. "'We Are Not What We Seem': Rethinking Black Working-Class Opposition in the Jim Crow South." *Journal of American History* 80 (June 1993): 75–112.

———. *Race Rebels: Culture, Politics, and the Black Working Class.* New York: Free Press, 1994.

King, Corretta Scott. *My Life with Martin Luther King, Jr.* New York: Hodder and Stoughton, 1969.

King, Martin Luther, Jr. *Stride Toward Freedom: The Montgomery Story.* New York: Harper and Row, 1958.

———. *Strength to Love.* Philadelphia: Fortress Press, 1963.

King, Mary. *Freedom Song: A Personal Story of the 1960s Civil Rights Movement.* New York: William Morrow, 1987.

King, Richard. *Civil Rights and the Idea of Freedom.* Oxford: Oxford University Press, 1992.

Kirk, John. *Redefining the Color Line: Black Activism in Little Rock, Arkansas, 1940–70.* Gainesville: University Press of Florida, 2002.

———. "State of the Art: Martin Luther King., Jr." *Journal of American Studies* 38 (2004): 329–47.

Kunstler, William and Sheila Isenberg. *My Life as a Radical Lawyer.* New York: Carol Publishing, 1994.

Lawson, Steven. "Freedom Then, Freedom Now: The Historiography of the Civil Rights Movement." *The American Historical Review* 96 (April 1991): 456–71.

Lentz, Richard. *Symbols, the News Magazines, and Martin Luther King.* Baton Rouge: Louisiana State University Press, 1990.

Levine, Lawrence. *Black Culture and Black Consciousness: Afro-American Folk Thought from Slavery to Freedom.* New York: Oxford University Press, 1977.

Levy, Peter. *Let Freedom Ring: A Documentary History of the Civil Rights Movement.* New York: Greenwood, 1992.

Lewis, David. *King: A Biography.* Chicago: University of Illinois Press, 1978.

Lewis, George. *Massive Resistance: The White Response to the Civil Rights Movement.* London: Hodder, 2006.

Lewis, John. *Walking with the Wind: A Memoir of the Movement.* New York: Simon and Schuster, 1998.

Lichtenstein, Alex. "'That Disposition to Theft, With Which They Have Been Branded': Moral Economy, Slave Management, and the Law." *Journal of Social History* 21 (Spring 1988): 413–40.

———. "Good Roads and Chain Gangs in the Progressive South: 'The Negro Convict is a Slave.'" *Journal of Southern History* 59 (February 1993): 85–110.

———. *Twice the Work of Free Labor: The Political Economy of Convict Labor in the New South*. London: Verso, 1996.

Ling, Peter and Sharon Montieth, eds. *Gender in the Civil Rights Movement*. New Brunswick: Rutgers, 2004.

———. "Uneasy Alliance: The NAACP and Martin Luther King." In *Long Is the Way and Hard: One Hundred Years of the NAACP*, edited by Kevern Verney and Lee Sartain, 43–58. Fayetteville: University of Arkansas Press, 2009.

Lipman, David M. "Mississippi's Prison Experience." *Mississippi Law Journal* 45, no. 3 (1974): 685–755.

Lomax, Alan. *The Land Where the Blues Began*. London: Minerva, 1994.

Lomax, Alan, and J. Lomax. *American Ballads and Folk Songs*. New York: Macmillan, 1966.

Lyon, Danny. *Memories of the Southern Civil Rights Movement*. Chapel Hill: University of North Carolina Press, 1992.

Mancini, Matthew J. *One Dies, Get Another: Convict Leasing in the American South, 1866–1928*. Columbia: University of South Carolina Press, 1996.

Marable, Manning. *How Capitalism Underdeveloped Black America*. Boston: South End Press, 1983.

———. *Race, Reform, and Rebellion: The Second Reconstruction in Black America, 1945–1982*. London: MacMillan Press, 1984.

Marcus, Greil. *Mystery Train: Images of America in Rock 'n' Roll Music*. New York: E. P. Dutton, 1975.

Marsh, Charles. *God's Long Summer: Stories of Faith and Civil Rights*. Princeton: Princeton University Press, 1997.

Marshall, Burke. "The Protest Movement and the Law." *Virginia Law Review* 51: 785–803.

Martin, Charles. *The Angelo Herndon Case and Southern Justice*. Baton Rouge: Louisiana State University Press, 1976.

McAdam, Doug. *Freedom Summer*. New York: Oxford, 1988.

McCartney, John T. *Black Power Ideologies: An Essay in African-American Political Thought*. Philadelphia: Temple University Press, 1992.

McGuire, Danielle. "'It Was Like All of Us Had Been Raped': Sexual Violence, Community Mobilization, and the African American Freedom Struggle." *Journal of American History* 91 (December 2004): 906–31.

———. *At the Dark End of the Street: Black Women, Rape, and Resistance—A New History of the Civil Rights Movement from Rosa Parks to the Rise of Black Power*. New York: Alfred A. Knopf, 2010.

McMillen, Neil R. *Dark Journey: Black Mississippians in the Age of Jim Crow*. Urbana: University of Illinois Press, 1989.

McNeil, Genna Rae. "The Body, Sexuality, and Self-Defense in *State vs. Joan Little*, 1974–1975." *Journal of African American History* 93 (Spring 2008): 235–61.

Meier, August, and Elliott Rudwick. "The Boycott Movement Against Jim Crow Streetcars in the South, 1900–1906." *Journal of American History* 55 (March 1969): 756–75.

———. *CORE: A Study in the Civil Rights Movement, 1942–1968*. New York: Oxford University Press, 1973.

———. *Along the Color Line: Explorations in the Black Experience*. Urbana: University of Illinois Press, 1976.

Meier, August, and John H. Bracey. "The NAACP as a Reform Movement, 1909–1965: To Reach the Conscience of America." *Journal of Southern History* 59 (February 1993): 3–30.

Miller, Keith. *Voice of Deliverance: The Language of Martin Luther King, Jr., and Its Sources*. New York: Free Press, 1992.

Miller, Vivien. *Crime, Sexual Violence, and Clemency: Florida's Pardon Board and Penal System in the Progressive Era*. Gainesville: University Press of Florida, 2001.

Mills, Kay. *This Little Light of Mine*. New York: Dutton, 1993.

Mills, Nicholas. *Like a Holy Crusade: Mississippi, 1964—The Turning of the Civil Rights Movement in America*. Chicago: Ivan R. Dee, 1992.

Moody, Anne. *Coming of Age in Mississippi*. New York: Bantam, 1965.

Moore, Christopher. *Fighting for America: Black Soldiers—The Unsung Heroes of World War II*. New York: Ballantine Books, 2005.

Morris, Aldon D. *The Origins of the Civil Rights Movement: Black Communities Organizing for Change*. New York: Free Press, 1984.

Moses, Greg. *Revolution of Conscience: Martin Luther King, Jr., and the Philosophy of Nonviolence*. New York: Guilford Press, 1997.

Myers, Martha A. *Race, Labor, and Punishment in the New South*. Columbus: Ohio State University Press, 1998.

Myrdal, Gunnar. *An American Dilemma: The Negro Problem and Modern Democracy*. New York: Harper and Row, 1962.

Network of Black Organizers. *Black Prison Movements USA*. Trenton, New Jersey: Africa World Press, 1995.

Newton, Huey P., and J. Herman Blake. *Revolutionary Suicide*. London: Wildwood House, 1974.

———. "War Against the Panthers: A Study of Repression in America." Ph.D. dissertation, University of California at Santa Cruz, 1980.

Newton, Huey P., and Toni Morrison. *To Die for the People: The Writings of Huey P. Newton*. New York: Writers and Readers Publishing, 1995.

Nieman, Donald G. "Black Political Power and Criminal Justice: Washington County, Texas, 1868–1884." *Journal of Southern History* 50 (August 1989): 391–420.

———. "African American Communities, Politics, and Justice: Washington County, Texas, 1865–1890." In *Local Matters: Race, Crime, and Justice in the Nineteenth-Century South*, edited by Christopher Waldrep and Donald G. Nieman, 201–24. Athens: University of Georgia Press, 2001.

Oates, Stephen B. *Let the Trumpet Sound: A Life of Martin Luther King, Jr.* New York: Harpers and Row, 1994.

O'Brien, Gail Williams. *The Color of the Law: Race, Violence, and Justice in the Post-World War II South*. Chapel Hill: University of North Carolina Press, 1999.

Ogbar, Jeffrey. *Black Power: Radical Politics and African American Identity*. Baltimore: Johns Hopkins University Press, 2005.

Olson, Lynne. *Freedom's Daughters: The Unsung Heroines of the Civil Rights Movement from 1830 to 1970*. New York: Touchstone, 2001.

Oppenheimer, Martin. "The Southern Student Movement: Year 1." *Journal of Negro Education* 33 (Autumn 1964): 398–99.

———, ed. *The Sit-In Movement of 1960*. New York: Carlson, 1989.

Orange, David. *From Segregation to Civil Rights and Beyond: A Story of the Southland*. Frederick, Maryland: PublishAmerica, 2005.

O'Reilly, Kenneth. *"Racial Matters": The FBI's Secret File on Black America, 1960–1972*. New York: Free Press, 1989.

Oshinsky, David. *Worse than Slavery: Parchman Farm and the Ordeal of Jim Crow Justice*. New York: Free Press, 1996.

Parks, Rosa. *Rosa Parks: My Story*. New York: Puffin Books, 1992.

Payne, Charles. "Men Led, but Women Organized: Movement Participation of Women in the Mississippi Delta." In *Women in the Civil Rights Movement: Trailblazers and Torchbearers, 1941–1965*, edited by Vicki Crawford, Jacqueline Rouse, and Barbara Woods, 1–13. Brooklyn: Carlson, 1990.

———. *I've Got the Light of Freedom. The Organizing Tradition and the Mississippi Freedom Struggle*. Berkeley: University of California Press, 1995.

Pfeffer, Paula. "A. Philip Randolph: A Case Study in Black Leadership." Vol. 1. Ph.D. dissertation, Northwestern University, 1980.

Rabinowitz, Howard. "The Conflict between Blacks and the Police in the Urban South." *Historian* 39 (November 1976): 62–75.

———. *Race Relations in the Urban South, 1865–1890*. New York: Oxford University Press, 1980.

Raines, Howell, ed. *My Soul Is Rested: The Story of the Civil Rights Movement in the Deep South*. New York: Penguin, 1977.

Raper, Arthur F. *The Tragedy of Lynching*. Montclair, New Jersey: Patterson Smith, 1933.

Reagon, Bernice J. "Songs of the Civil Rights Movement, 1955–1965: A Study in Culture History." Ph.D. dissertation, Howard University, 1975.

Reddy, T. J. *Less Than a Score, But a Point*. New York: Vintage, 1974.

Riches, William T. Martin. *The Civil Rights Movement: Struggle and Resistance*. London: Macmillan, 1997.

Rise, Eric W. "Race, Rape, and Radicalism: The Case of the Martinsville Seven, 1949–1951." *Journal of Southern History* 58 (August 1992): 461–90.

Roberts, John. *From Trickster to Badman: The Black Folk Hero in Slavery and Freedom*. Philadelphia: University of Pennsylvania Press, 1989.

Robinson, Jo Ann Gibson. *The Montgomery Bus Boycott and the Women Who Started It: The Memoir of Jo Ann Gibson Robinson*. Knoxville: University of Tennessee Press, 1987.

Robinson, Jo Ann Ooiman. *Abraham Went Out: A Biography of A. J. Muste*. Philadelphia: Temple University Press, 1981.

Ryan, Yvonne. "Leading From the Back: Roy Wilkins's Leadership of the NAACP." In *Long Is the Way and Hard: One Hundred Years of the NAACP*, edited by Kevern Verney and Lee Sartain, 43–58. Fayetteville: University of Arkansas Press, 2009.

Salter, John. *Jackson, Mississippi: An American Chronicle of Struggle and Schism*. Hicksville, New York: Exposition Press, 1979.

Sanger, Kerran L. *When the Spirit Says Sing!: The Role of Freedom Songs in the Civil Rights Movement*. New York City: Garland, 1995.

Schlanger, Margo. "Beyond the Hero Judge: Institutional Reform Litigation as Litigation." *Michigan Law Review* 97 (1999): 1,994–2,036.

Schutz, Christopher. "'Going to Hell to Get the Devil': The 'Charlotte Three' Case and the Decline of Grassroots Activism in 1970s Charlotte, North Carolina." Ph.D. dissertation, University of Georgia, 1999.

Seale, Bobby. *A Lonely Rage: The Autobiography of Bobby Seale*. New York: Times Books, 1978.

Sellers, Cleveland. *The River of No Return: The Autobiography of a Black Militant and the Life and Death of SNCC*. Jackson: University Press of Mississippi, 1990.

Shapiro, Herbert. *White Violence and Black Response: From Reconstruction to Montgomery*. Amherst: University of Massachusetts Press, 1988.

Shapiro, Karin A. *A New South Rebellion: The Battle Against Convict Labor in the*

Tennessee Coalfields, 1871–1896. Chapel Hill: University of North Carolina Press, 1998.

Sibley, Mulford, and Philip Jacob. *Conscription of Conscience: The American State and the Conscientious Objector, 1940–1947*. Ithaca: Cornell, 1952.

Sitkoff, Harvard. "Racial Militancy and Interracial Violence in the Second World War." *Journal of American History* 58 (December 1971): 661–81.

Sloop, John M. *The Cultural Prison: Discourse, Prisoners, and Punishment*. Tuscaloosa: University of Alabama Press, 1996.

Smead, Howard. *Blood Justice: The Lynching of Mack Charles Parker*. New York: Oxford University Press, 1986.

Smith, Albert C. "'Southern Violence' Reconsidered: Arson as Protest in Black-Belt Georgia, 1865–1910." *Journal of Southern History* 51 (November 1985): 527–64.

Sullivan, Andrea D. "Politicization: The Effect of the Nation of Islam Upon the Prison Inmate Culture." Ph.D. dissertation, University of Pennsylvania, 1976.

Sullivan, Patricia. *Days of Hope: Race and Democracy in the New Deal Era*. Chapel Hill: University of North Carolina Press, 1996.

Taylor, William Banks. *Down on Parchman Farm: The Great Prison in the Mississippi Delta*. Columbus: Ohio State University Press, 1999.

Tolnay, Stewart E., and E. M. Beck. "Lethal Social Control in the South: Lynchings and Executions Between 1880 and 1930." In *Inequality and Social Control*, by George S. Bridges and Martha A. Myers, 176–94. Boulder, Colo.: Westview Press, 1994.

Tracy, J. R. "Forging Dissent in an Age of Consensus: Radical Pacifism in America, 1940 to 1970." Ph.D. dissertation, Stanford University, 1993.

Tuck, Stephen. *Beyond Atlanta: The Struggle for Racial Equality in Georgia, 1940–80*. Athens: University of Georgia Press, 2001.

Tyson, Timothy B. "Robert F. Williams, 'Black Power,' and the Roots of the African American Freedom Struggle." *Journal of American History* 85 (September 1998): 540–70.

———. *Radio Free Dixie: Robert F. Williams and the Roots of Black Power*. Chapel Hill: University of North Carolina Press, 1999.

Useem, Bert, and Peter Kimball. *States of Siege: U.S. Prison Riots, 1971–1986*. Oxford: Oxford University Press, 1989.

Van Deburg, William L. *New Day in Babylon: The Black Power Movement and American Culture, 1965–1975*. Chicago: University of Chicago Press, 1992.

Verney, Kevern, and Lee Sartain, eds. *Long Is the Way and Hard: One Hundred Years of the NAACP*. Fayetteville: University of Arkansas Press, 2009.

Waldrep, Christopher. *Roots of Disorder: Race and Criminal Justice in the American South, 1817–80*. Urbana: University of Illinois Press, 1998.

———. "War of Words: The Controversy Over the Definition of Lynching, 1899–1940." *Journal of Southern History* 66 (February 2000): 75–100.

Waldrep, Christopher, and Donald G. Nieman, eds. *Local Matters: Race, Crime, and Justice in the Nineteenth-Century South*. Athens: University of Georgia Press, 2001.

Walker, Jenny. "Black Violence and Nonviolence in the Civil Rights and Black Power Eras." Ph.D. dissertation, University of Newcastle upon Tyne, 2000.

Watters, Pat. *Down to Now: Reflections on the Southern Civil Rights Movement*. Athens: University of Georgia Press, 1971.

White, Robert M. "The Tallahassee Sit-Ins and CORE: A Nonviolent Revolutionary Submovement." Ph.D. dissertation, Florida State University, 1974.

White, Walter. *Rope and Faggot: A Biography of Judge Lynch*. New York: Alfred A. Knopf, 1929.

Widell, Robert W., Jr. "'The Power Belongs to Us and We Belong to the Revolutionary Age': The Alabama Black Liberation Front and the Long Reach of the Black Panther Party." In *Liberated Territory: Untold Local Perspectives on the Black Panther Party*, edited by Yohuru Williams and Jama Lazerow, 136–80. Durham: Duke University Press, 2008.

Wilkins, Roy, and Tom Mathews. *Standing Fast: The Autobiography of Roy Wilkins*. New York: Viking Press, 1982.

Williams, Yohuru, and Jama Lazerow, eds. *Liberated Territory: Untold Local Perspectives on the Black Panther Party*. Durham: Duke University Press, 2008.

Wittner, Lawrence. *Rebels Against War: The American Peace Movement, 1941–1960*. New York: Columbia University Press, 1969.

Wolff, Miles. *Lunch at the 5 & 10*. Chicago: Ivan R. Dee, 1970.

Wright, Erik Olin, ed. *The Politics of Punishment: A Critical Analysis of Prisons in America*. New York: Harper and Colophon, 1973.

Wright, George C. *Racial Violence in Kentucky, 1865–1940: Lynchings, Mob Rule, and 'Legal Lynchings.'* Baton Rouge: Louisiana State University Press, 1990.

Wynn, Neil. *The Afro-American and the Second World War*. New York: Holmes and Meier, 1993.

Young, Andrew. *A Way Out of No Way: The Spiritual Memoirs of Andrew Young*. Nashville: Thomas Nelson, 1994.

Zangrando, Robert L. *The NAACP Crusade Against Lynching, 1909–1950*. Philadelphia: Temple University Press, 1980.

Zinn, Howard. *SNCC: The New Abolitionists*. Boston: Beacon Press, 1965.

Index

Zoe Colley is lecturer in American history at the University of Dundee, Scotland.

*   *   *

The University Press of Florida is the scholarly publishing agency for the State University System of Florida, comprising Florida A&M University, Florida Atlantic University, Florida Gulf Coast University, Florida International University, Florida State University, New College of Florida, University of Central Florida, University of Florida, University of North Florida, University of South Florida, and University of West Florida.

NEW PERSPECTIVES ON THE HISTORY OF THE SOUTH
Edited by John David Smith

"In the Country of the Enemy": The Civil War Reports of a Massachusetts Corporal, edited by William C. Harris (1999)

The Wild East: A Biography of the Great Smoky Mountains, by Margaret L. Brown (2000; first paperback edition, 2001)

Crime, Sexual Violence, and Clemency: Florida's Pardon Board and Penal System in the Progressive Era, by Vivien M. L. Miller (2000)

The New South's New Frontier: A Social History of Economic Development in Southwestern North Carolina, by Stephen Wallace Taylor (2001)

Redefining the Color Line: Black Activism in Little Rock, Arkansas, 1940–1970, by John A. Kirk (2002)

The Southern Dream of a Caribbean Empire, 1854–1861, by Robert E. May (2002)

Forging a Common Bond: Labor and Environmental Activism during the BASF Lockout, by Timothy J. Minchin (2003)

Dixie's Daughters: The United Daughters of the Confederacy and the Preservation of Confederate Culture, by Karen L. Cox (2003)

The Other War of 1812: The Patriot War and the American Invasion of Spanish East Florida, by James G. Cusick (2003)

"Lives Full of Struggle and Triumph": Southern Women, Their Institutions, and Their Communities, edited by Bruce L. Clayton and John A. Salmond (2003)

German-Speaking Officers in the United States Colored Troops, 1863–1867, by Martin W. Öfele (2004)

Southern Struggles: The Southern Labor Movement and the Civil Rights Struggle, by John A. Salmond (2004)

Radio and the Struggle for Civil Rights in the South, by Brian Ward (2004; first paperback edition, 2006)

Luther P. Jackson and a Life for Civil Rights, by Michael Dennis (2004)

Southern Ladies, New Women: Race, Region, and Clubwomen in South Carolina, 1890–1930, by Joan Marie Johnson (2004)

Fighting Against the Odds: A Concise History of Southern Labor Since World War II, by Timothy J. Minchin (2004; first paperback edition, 2006)

"Don't Sleep With Stevens!": The J. P. Stevens Campaign and the Struggle to Organize the South, 1963–1980, by Timothy J. Minchin (2005)

"The Ticket to Freedom": The NAACP and the Struggle for Black Political Integration, by Manfred Berg (2005; first paperback edition, 2007)

"War Governor of the South": North Carolina's Zeb Vance in the Confederacy, by Joe A. Mobley (2005)

Planters' Progress: Modernizing Confederate Georgia, by Chad Morgan (2005)

The Officers of the CSS Shenandoah, by Angus Curry (2006)

The Rosenwald Schools of the American South, by Mary S. Hoffschwelle (2006)

Honor in Command: Lt. Freeman S. Bowley's Civil War Service in the 30th United States Colored Infantry, edited by Keith Wilson (2006)

A Black Congressman in the Age of Jim Crow: South Carolina's George Washington Murray, by John F. Marszalek (2006)

The Spirit and the Shotgun: Armed Resistance and the Struggle for Civil Rights, by Simon Wendt (2007; first paperback edition, 2010)

Making a New South: Race, Leadership, and Community after the Civil War, edited by Paul A. Cimbala and Barton C. Shaw (2007)

From Rights to Economics: The Ongoing Struggle for Black Equality in the U.S. South, by Timothy J. Minchin (2008)

Slavery on Trial: Race, Class, and Criminal Justice in Antebellum Richmond, Virginia, by James M. Campbell (2008; first paperback edition, 2010)

Welfare and Charity in the Antebellum South, by Timothy James Lockley (2008; first paperback edition, 2009)

T. Thomas Fortune the Afro-American Agitator: A Collection of Writings, 1880–1928, by Shawn Leigh Alexander (2008; first paperback edition, 2010)

Francis Butler Simkins: A Life, by James S. Humphreys (2008)

Black Manhood and Community Building in North Carolina, 1900–1930, by Angela Hornsby-Gutting (2009; first paperback edition, 2010)

Counterfeit Gentlemen: Manhood and Humor in the Old South, by John Mayfield (2009; first paperback edition, 2010)

The Southern Mind Under Union Rule: The Diary of James Rumley, Beaufort, North Carolina, 1862–1865, edited by Judkin Browning (2009; first paperback edition, 2011)

The Quarters and the Fields: Slave Families in the Non-Cotton South, by Damian Alan Pargas (2010; first paperback edition, 2011)

The Door of Hope: Republican Presidents and the First Southern Strategy, 1877–1933, by Edward O. Frantz (2011; first paperback edition, 2012)

Painting Dixie Red: When, Where, Why, and How the South Became Republican, edited by Glenn Feldman (2011)

After Freedom Summer: How Race Realigned Mississippi Politics, 1965–1986, by Chris Danielson (2011; first paperback edition, 2013)

Dreams and Nightmares: Martin Luther King Jr., Malcolm X, and the Struggle for Black Equality in America, by Britta Waldschmidt-Nelson (2012)

Hard Labor and Hard Time: Florida's "Sunshine Prison" and Chain Gangs, by Vivien M. L. Miller (2012)

Ain't Scared of Your Jail: Arrest, Imprisonment, and the Civil Rights Movement, by Zoe A. Colley (2013; first paperback edition, 2014)

After Slavery: Race, Labor, and Citizenship in the Reconstruction South, edited by Bruce E. Baker and Brian Kelly (2013)

Stinking Stones and Rocks of Gold: Phosphate, Fertilizer, and Industrialization in Postbellum South Carolina, by Shepherd W. McKinley (2014)

The Path to the Greater, Freer, Truer World: Southern Civil Rights and Anticolonialism, 1937–1955, by Lindsey R. Swindall (2014)

www.ingramcontent.com/pod-product-compliance
Lightning Source LLC
Chambersburg PA
CBHW021505090426
42739CB00007B/475